QUESTI
DIVORCE AND REMARRIAGE

Questions About Divorce and Remarriage

ANDREW CORNES

MONARCH
BOOKS
Mill Hill, London

Scripture quotations from the Holy Bible, *New
International Version,* copyright © 1973, 1978, 1984 by the
International Bible Society. Used by permission of Hodder and
Stoughton Ltd. The *Revised Standard Version* and *New Revised
Standard Version,* copyright 1946, 1952, 1971 and 1973
by the Division of Christian Education of the
National Council of Churches of Christ
in the United States of America.

British Library Cataloguing Data
A catalogue record for this book is available
from the British Library.

Designed and produced by Bookprint Creative Services
P.O. Box 827, BN21 3YJ, England for
MONARCH BOOKS
in association with
ANGUS HUDSON LTD
Concorde House, Grenville Place, Mill Hill
London, NW7 3SA.
Printed in Great Britain.

CONTENTS

CHAPTER 1

THE GENTLE TRUTH-TELLER

Richard had recently started coming to church. He stopped me after a Sunday service: 'Tell me about the Discovery Course. What is it?' Over a cup of coffee, I explained that it's a course which looks at the core beliefs of the Christian faith; it's designed for those who are thinking seriously about Christianity or who have recently discovered Christian faith for themselves.

After we'd talked for a while, it was my turn to ask a question: 'What made you interested in the course in the first place?'

Richard told me immediately that he was divorced. They had separated eighteen months beforehand, and the divorce had come through within the last six months. Initially, he had allowed his world to close in. He had worked ridiculously long hours and then come home and watched TV until he was so tired that he knew he would sleep. He hardly saw anyone apart from at work.

But one or two friends stayed in touch and urged him to get involved in something outside work and home. He had wondered about taking up hockey again or an evening class in car mechanics. But then he got talking to a colleague who was also divorced and who said that through the pain of his own divorce he had 'found Jesus Christ'. The man was obviously sincere, he had clearly got his life together again and his faith seemed genuine.

Richard felt it would be worth taking a serious look at the Christian faith himself. He joined the Discovery Course. The first evening was entitled: 'Who is this Jesus?' Different passages from the Bible were explored, all to do with Jesus Christ.

Richard started his search in the right place: with Jesus Christ. The New Testament focuses on Christ. The Old Testament also speaks about Christ, prophesying the kind of person he would be. One famous prophecy is Isaiah 42:1-4. God is speaking about the Christ who will come:

> Here is my servant, whom I uphold,
>   my chosen one in whom I delight;
> I will put my Spirit on him
>   and he will bring justice to the nations.
> He will not shout or cry out,
>   or raise his voice in the streets.
> A bruised reed he will not break,
>   and a smouldering wick he will not snuff out.
> In faithfulness he will bring forth justice;
>   he will not falter or be discouraged
> till he establishes justice on earth.
>   In his law the islands will put their hope.

The New Testament writers were clear that this is a prophecy of Jesus Christ. There are echoes of it in several places when they write about Christ and it is quoted extensively in Matthew 12:15-21. What does it tell us about the founder of Christianity in whom Richard was beginning to be interested and to whom many others affected by divorce and remarriage look for support and answers to their questions?

1. He brings the truth

The central statement of the passage is translated by the New International Version: 'He will bring justice to the nations' (v. 1). It is clear that this is central because it is repeated, in only slightly different form, in verse 3: 'In faithfulness he will bring forth justice' and verse 4: 'He will not falter . . . till he establishes justice on earth'.

The Hebrew word can indeed mean 'justice' but it is probably a misleading translation here. It suggests in modern English the righting of legal wrongs or the establishing of a just, rather than a corrupt, government (the very thing which his contemporaries wrongly hoped from Jesus – see John 6:14,15; Acts 1:6). It's a very common Hebrew word in the Old Testament and is variously translated as 'law' (e.g. Exodus 21:1; Psalm 119:13), 'ordinance' (e.g. Psalm 81:4), 'requirement' (e.g. Jeremiah 5:4, 5), and in other ways. The best translation here is probably 'God's (or Christ's) truth'. It is, however, not simply truth to be grasped with the mind but truth to be acted on.

Here then is the mission given by God to Christ on which Isaiah 42:1-4 concentrates: 'He will bring truth to the nations' (v. 1); 'in faithfulness he will bring forth truth' (v. 3); 'he will not falter . . . till he establishes truth on earth' (v. 4).

This book is addressed to those who have questions; specifically those who have questions about extremely difficult marriage relationships, about separation and divorce, and about remarriage. It is addressed to those, like Richard, who believe they may find the answers in and from Jesus Christ.

Isaiah assures us we have come to the right place. A central part of Christ's mission was to bring God's truth, the truth to accept and live by in every area of our life. That will certainly include the vital areas of marriage and divorce.

The questions asked in this book are those which I have heard most often when people talk about divorce and remarriage and which various divorced people have urged me to include in the book; many of them are as old as time itself when the first accusations by marriage partners began (Genesis 3:11,12).

The answers are quarried from the Bible* and especially from the teaching of Jesus. Since he brings God's truth, we need to listen to him.

2. He cares for truth in national life

Jesus' mission is not just to individuals, it is also to nations. This is made clear from the beginning: 'He will bring truth to the nations' (v. 1). And it is repeated at the end of the passage: 'He will not falter . . . till he establishes truth on earth' (v. 4) ('earth' here means the whole inhabited world). The last phrase is: 'In his law the islands will put their hope' (v. 4); to the land-bound Israelites, 'islands' meant the farthest parts of the earth.

Isaiah's main point was that the truth which previously had been known only to Israel would now be brought to Gentile nations as well. But it also shows that Christ is not simply interested in 'seeking and saving lost' individuals (Luke 19:10) but also in 'establishing truth' in national life (Isaiah 42:1,4).

Marriage breakdown, divorce and remarriage are now in-grained features of our national life. They affect every person; they affect every marriage. More than one in three marriages in England and Wales now ends in divorce; and the divorce rate, having remained stable for most of the 1980s, is beginning to rise again. Most people actively encourage divorcees to remarry, even though the failure rate of second and third marriages is considerably higher than for first marriages.

Changes in society's view of divorce and remarriage, and 'establishing God's truth' about marriage in our national life, are

* I have quoted normally from the New International Version. Where another translation is indicated it is because it gives a more literal translation of the original Hebrew or Greek.

outside the scope of this small book. But they are not outside the scope of Christ's concern or Christ's mission. He cares deeply about education for marriage by parents and in schools and youth groups; about the preparation of engaged couples for marriage by their families, through churches and through secular agencies; about family and divorce law; about marriage guidance and conciliation services; about the marital and sexual values expressed in and disseminated through TV soaps, plays, discussions and comedies.

3. He cares for the bruised individual

But Christ's concern is not only for the nation; it is for the individual too, and particularly the bruised individual: 'A bruised reed he will not break, and a smouldering wick he will not snuff out' (v. 3).

One of the most characteristic features of the God of the Bible, and of the Christ who is his Son, is that they are particularly concerned with the disadvantaged: those who are single after being married, those without one or both parents and those who suffer. It is therefore not at all surprising that Christ's mission is particularly to the 'bruised reed' and the 'smouldering wick'. To Christ every person is valuable, even the 'bruised reed' whom others would throw out as useless and the 'smouldering wick' whom others would regard as worth nothing any more.

It is the bruised for whom this book is written: people whose experience of marriage is that it has crushed them rather than enriched them, and destroyed them rather than built them up. It is very normal in these circumstances to feel utterly useless, unable to take on any extra responsibility, failing in those responsibilities which cannot be avoided – a bruised reed.

It is equally normal to find that your spiritual life is at a very low ebb; the spiritual flame has almost gone out – a smouldering wick. You feel sometimes, perhaps often, that you are no good to anyone, least of all God.

Isaiah states firmly that Jesus cares for you – for you especially. He has no intention of declaring you useless and finally 'breaking' you. He does not despise your almost extinguished faith and has not the remotest inclination to 'snuff it out'.

Isaac Watts' hymn catches the truth of these verses superbly:

> He'll never quench the smoking flax,
> But raise it to a flame.
> The bruised reed he never breaks,
> Nor scorns the meanest name.

If you are feeling bruised, Christ is the very person to turn to.

4. He is prepared to take time

It takes time to heal deep bruises and to coax a flame back to full life. But Christ is determined to take that time.

This is already shown in Isaiah 42:2 – 'He will not shout or cry out, or raise his voice in the streets.' When a new king succeeded to the throne in the Ancient Near East, it was the custom for him to re-enact the laws and have them proclaimed in public.[1] Others, whether kings or leading government officers, would impose their will violently and peremptorily. But Christ, as Isaiah prophesied, was no tyrant, no dictator or demagogue. He prefers to work quietly and steadily.

This means working to a much longer time-scale. Verses 3 and 4 bring this out very clearly: 'In faithfulness he will bring forth truth; he will not falter or be discouraged till he establishes truth on earth.' The implication is that a lesser person might have become discouraged; the task of 'establishing truth' is not accomplished easily or in a minute.

There is a Hebrew play on words here which is hard to bring out in English: 'Falter' (v. 4) is the same basic word as 'smouldering' (v. 3), and 'be discouraged' (v. 4) is the same root word as 'bruised' (v. 3). My translation attempts to bring this out: 'A crushed reed he will not break, and a low-burning wick he will not extinguish . . . He will not burn low and he will not be crushed until he establishes truth on the earth' (vv. 3,4).

In other words, it is not only we who are under attack. So is Christ; he has enemies, he has set-backs. The difference between him and us is that his determination and confidence don't weaken. North translates verse 4: 'With faith undimmed and spirit unbroken he will establish my [God's] law in the world.' [2] Christ is therefore the right person to turn to for support, courage and healing.

This picture of Christ's work in our lives taking time, and experiencing set-backs, is very realistic. Many of us find it extraordinarily difficult in a largely loveless marriage to stay true to our marriage vows. Recovery from divorce is a long, uphill struggle, during which we fall in a heap many times. Seeking reconciliation after separation or even divorce raises our hopes and often dashes them again. In all these areas it is two steps forward and one and a half back. It is enough to put anyone off.

But it is not enough to put Christ off. 'The intention [of verses 3 and 4] is not to say that [Christ] will be immune from suffering but only that the pressures and blows that immobilise others will not deter him. They will, rather, find him with adequate inner resources ("not falter") and with a resilience against outward blows ("not . . . be discouraged").' [3]

This book expresses the conviction that Christ can gently fan into flame marriages that have almost gone out, can forge a new, fulfilling life for the person devastated by separation and divorce, can bring about reconciliation where there seemed to be only anger and contempt. As you read it, you may well be tempted sometimes to think: 'This could never be true for me.'

Some of it may not ever come true; reconciliation, for example, needs two people willing to work at it. But all that is stated in this book may come true and, in many lives, has come true. That is because it is Christ who has given the promises quoted in this book and because Christ is at work in our lives.

But we must give him time. The wounds are deep. Normally it will take many years for Christ to heal them. That is his way. We must not give up in impatience but allow him the time that he needs.

5. His truth fulfils the world's hopes

The last phrase is best translated: 'And the coastlands [or: islands] wait for [or: hope for] his law' (v. 4, RSV). We have already seen that the 'islands' meant to the Hebrews the remotest parts of the earth. They, says Isaiah, are eagerly waiting for the truth that Christ will bring.

Before Christ came there was no real hope for the world: 'Remember that formerly you who are Gentiles by birth . . . were separate from Christ . . . without hope and without God in the world' (Ephesians 2:11,12). And yet there was in everyone, and there is now for those who are not yet Christians, a diffuse longing: there must be something better, there must be more to life than this. Isaiah is not saying that the nations knew what they were longing for, but that their obscure hopes and longings find their fulfilment in the 'law' – the teaching – that Christ brings.

When your marriage breaks up, it can seem as if there is no point in living any more. It is not uncommon to attempt suicide; it is normal to feel that life is just dragging on in a meaningless way. Yet even then we catch glimmers of hope. Especially as the months go on, we begin to feel there may be some answers to our questions and that there may be ways to reconstruct a healthy, fulfilled life and even to rebuild the ruins of a shattered marriage.

There are. Isaiah says that it is Christ and his teaching that we are feeling after, whether we are aware of it or not. It is 'his law', and his law alone, that will fulfil our yearning for meaning and direction (v. 4).

But it is his 'law' (v. 4) and his 'truth' (vv. 1,3,4). We cannot just come to Christ for his comfort and his reassuring presence. He offers both of these of course, but he offers them to those who will accept and act on his teaching. It is that teaching – the only true fulfilment of the world's hopes, and the divorcee's hopes – which this book seeks to present.

And that is why I have called this first chapter 'The Gentle Truth-teller'. There is no question that Jesus is gentle with us: he will not break a bruised reed, he will strengthen it; he will not snuff out a smouldering wick but carefully trim it until it gives out a steady, bright light. But the way that he does this is by bringing us his truth, often taking many years to help us assimilate, and act upon, his teaching which is sometimes uncomfortable but always ultimately strengthening.

Key verses

Jesus said: 'Come to me, all you who are weary and burdened, and I will give you rest. Take my yoke upon you and learn from me' (Matthew 11:28,29).

CHAPTER 2

QUESTIONS ABOUT GOD'S GUIDANCE

Rachel is a single woman in her late thirties, who met and fell in love with a divorcee. She asked to talk with me: 'I used to believe it was wrong to remarry after divorce; but I've had to think it through again since meeting Paul, and now I'm not so sure. His wife was mentally unstable and it was she who insisted on the divorce; Paul was trying to keep the marriage together. I've talked to several Christians and they don't seem to agree. I'm confused.'

Rachel, and all of us who want to know what God thinks about divorce or remarriage, have questions about God's will and God's guidance.

How do I discover God's will about divorce or remarriage?

If we are Christians, we seek to follow the teaching of Jesus Christ. The most important question for us on any issue will be: 'What did Jesus teach about this subject?'

One of the earliest ways to express Christian faith was to say: 'Jesus is Lord' (see Romans 10:9; 1 Corinthians 12:3). We are his servants; he is to be Lord of every area of our lives, including our mind (what we think) and our behaviour (what we do). It must be right, then, that we should receive our understanding of all life, including marriage and divorce, from him.

Jesus himself made this point to his disciples. On the night before he died, he said to them: 'You call me "Teacher" and "Lord", and rightly so, for that is what I am' (John 13:13). He went on to give them some specific teaching about sacrificial service, and then added: 'Now that you know these things, you will be blessed if you do them' (John 13:17).

In fact, God himself made the same point to some of Christ's disciples when they were confused. On the Mount of Transfiguration, when Jesus' glory shone through and Elijah and Moses appeared, Peter blurted out a bewildered suggestion that they should make three tents. Mark comments: 'He did not know what to say, they were so frightened.' God's voice then came to the disciples out of a cloud: 'This is my Son, whom I love [Matthew's account adds: 'With him I am well pleased.']. Listen to him!' (Mark 9:2-7; Matthew 17:1-5). Christ's followers, instead of making their own suggestions for what might be right, need to listen to him.

Fortunately, Jesus taught on a number of occasions about divorce and remarriage. In fact, most of the New Testament material on this subject is found in the Gospels.

Clearly his teaching about remarriage and divorce was treasured. Paul very rarely referred directly to the teaching of Jesus while he was on earth, but on this subject he deliberately quotes what Jesus taught (1 Corinthians 7:10,11).

Christian leaders disagree. Whom should I believe?

The trouble is, as Rachel pointed out, that Christians don't agree about divorce and remarriage. One clergyman encourages a divorce when all love seems to have drained out of the marriage; another says it would be wrong. One book tells Rachel it would be against God's will to marry someone like Paul who's already been married; another book assures her that it is fine to go ahead. The Methodists agree to marriage services for divorcees; the Anglicans (for the most part) do not. And sometimes the 'ordinary' Christian can feel bewildered, caught in the middle between 'experts' who disagree.

It is true that there are disagreements, although the extent of the disagreement can be overstated. Certainly among those who seek to listen to, and put into practice, the teaching of Christ and of the New Testament there is agreement on many questions that relate to divorce and remarriage. Nevertheless, we are confronted by conflicting views. How can we come to any clear conclusions?

The most important starting-point is to want to do God's will. There was an occasion when the Jews were questioning Christ's own teaching. Jesus replied: 'If any man's will is to do his [God's] will, he shall known whether the teaching is from God or whether I am speaking on my own authority' (John 7:17, RSV). This was the basic attitude needed, Jesus said, to evaluate his own teaching. We must want to do God's will, however hard it proves to be.

The same attitude is essential when we seek to evaluate a Christian leader's teaching, or a book's teaching, today. None of us come to this subject without our emotions being involved. All of us have vested interests in hearing and accepting one kind of teaching or another. And precisely because there is a danger of our 'accumulat[ing] for [our]selves teachers to suit [our] own likings' (2 Timothy 4:3, RSV), we need to be certain that our fundamental desire is to do God's will, wherever it may lead us.

It is very possible to hide behind disagreements. We hear some tough teaching, which we don't like, from one Christian leader, and we deliberately go and ask the advice of another leader, whose views we have reason to believe will be more lenient. Then we say that if the leaders can't agree, how can we be expected to know what God's will is? This lets us off the hook of wrestling with the teaching of Scripture and coming to our own humbly-held convictions.

But we cannot shirk that hard work. There is no evidence in the New Testament that Christians disagreed in the way we do over divorce and remarriage, but in connection with a different area of disagreement Paul says: 'Each one should be fully convinced in his own mind' (Romans 14:5). This is not at all the modern thought: 'It doesn't matter what you believe as long as you're sincere.' Rather, it is urging us to use our minds to think about what God has revealed and to work out its implications for our lives.

We are not independent individuals, free to decide as we choose. Instead, we are Christ's servants, answerable to our Master. It is Christ who decides whether in our thinking and behaviour we 'stand or fall' (Romans 14:4).

The Bible's culture was different from ours. Is its teaching on divorce and remarriage still relevant today?

But still that leaves us with questions about the Bible's teaching. Women, for instance, were economically and socially dependent on men in New Testament times. Perhaps it was primarily to protect them that Jesus spoke so forcefully against divorce and remarriage. If so, now that women are much more independent, perhaps there is no need to prohibit divorce and remarriage so sweepingly.

Or again, men and women lived far less long in the first century BC. If someone was divorced, he (or she) might not have many years left before he died; under these circumstances, it was not such a hardship to prohibit remarriage. But now that people marry young, divorce young and then may have another sixty years of life stretching before them, is it appropriate any more to forbid remarriage to divorcees?

As it happens, Jesus does say something about the difference between his own day and another period of history. This is striking because it is most unusual in his teaching. Again and again he quotes the teaching of the Old Testament and affirms that it accurately conveys the mind of God for Christians in the kingdom of God, just as much as for Israelites under the old covenant.

But on the question of divorce he departs from this practice. He agrees that 'Moses permitted you to divorce your wives' but says that it was 'because your hearts were hard'. Christ now clearly takes away that permission, except in one circumstance: 'I tell you that anyone who divorces his wife, except for marital unfaithfulness, and marries another woman commits adultery' (Matthew 19:8,9).

What is more, he traces this back to the way God originally created men and women 'at the beginning'. God created men and women so that he could 'join them together' in a marriage unity ('one flesh') which no man must separate (Matthew 19:4-8). Clearly Jesus views this original purpose of God for marriage, with its implications for divorce and remarriage, as binding on Christians in all subsequent ages, irrespective of cultural changes.

Can you make general rules? Isn't every case different?

But is any of Christ's teaching really binding? Should it really be regarded as a new law at all? Isn't it rather more like guidelines? On this understanding, Christ gives general principles in his teaching, ideals, but he never expected us to follow what he said to the letter in every case. Instead, we have to take these principles and apply them imaginatively and differently to each situation. So, for example, in some cases where the couple are sexually faithful but constantly row with each other, divorce will be wrong in Christ's eyes; in other cases it will be perfectly legitimate.

But in his most important section of teaching about divorce and remarriage (Matthew 19:1-12; Mark 10:1-12), Jesus is in fact being asked a question about the law: 'Is it lawful for a man to divorce his wife for any and every reason?' In Mark's account, he replies immediately by asking, 'What did Moses command you?' In other words: what is written in the Mosaic law?

He agrees with their assessment of the Mosaic law, but then quotes from the book of Genesis (also considered by the Jews to be part of 'the Law') to show what God's original and abiding will is. In answer to their original question ('Is it lawful. . .?'), he gives his ruling based on this Genesis passage: 'Therefore what God has joined together, let man not separate.' In Matthew's account, to underline the fact that he is giving a new law, or rather a reaffirmation of what God originally laid down as lawful and unlawful, he adds, 'I tell you that anyone who divorces his wife, except for marital unfaithfulness, and marries another woman commits adultery.'

These are not general guidelines, to be applied with plenty of exceptions and with freedom. This is his firm ruling, binding on all those who claim to follow him.

What weight should I give to the opinion of my friends?

When a woman like Rachel is thinking of marrying a divorcee, friends are often not slow to give advice. When a marriage is breaking up, while some friends don't know what to say and perhaps avoid you, others will be giving you their suggestions for your present situation and your future, whether you ask for it or not. And before that, while you are together, if friends know that you are going through difficulties, they may well give you their advice.

Some of this advice will wash over you and some may irritate you. But if you are going through the pain of separation and divorce, you may well be bewildered and not easily able to take decisions by yourself. What weight should you give to your friends' opinions?

Of course that will depend in part on how well they know you and can enter into your feelings and dilemmas. Certainly you need the support of friends; those who have recently experienced separation often make the mistake of shutting themselves away from all human contact. People who have been through separation and divorce themselves can be very helpful, especially in giving emotional support.

But with the great issues with which this book is concerned – when it may be right to separate or divorce; whether it could be right to remarry; whether it is God's will for a divorcee to remain single – we need to test carefully all the opinions we are offered, even by good friends. What makes them give us that advice? Where in the teaching of Jesus and the New Testament do they find that suggestion or that possibility?

There is a danger that friends, with the very best intentions, can lead us away from the will of God. It was surely because of his love for Jesus that Peter tried to dissuade him from going to the cross. But Jesus had to rebuke Peter sharply: 'Get behind me, Satan! You are a stumbling-block to me; you do not have in mind the things of God, but the things of men' (Matthew 16:23).

We naturally seek advice from those friends who are likely to tell us what we want to hear. The Bible warns us that this is dangerous: 'A man who flatters his neighbour spreads a net for his feet' (Proverbs 29:5, RSV). In fact, the people whom we most need to listen to are those friends who tell us uncomfortable truths: 'Faithful are the wounds of a friend; profuse are the kisses of an enemy' (Proverbs 27:6, RSV). They will not always be right, of course, but their words will always need to be weighed carefully.

But there is one friend whom we need to listen to above all others. And we are not only to pay attention to his words, but to obey them. He himself said, 'You are my friends if you do what I command' (John 15:14). His teaching must outweigh all other advice.

Many 'coincidences' seem to be drawing us together. Is that significant?

A couple came to see me; he was divorced and her husband had died in a car crash. Both were Christians and were trying to work out whether it would be right for them to marry. They found the biblical passages confusing, but as they were praying over the question and continuing their relationship, a number of 'coincidences' seemed to be encouraging them towards marriage.

For example, she had been praying about the question and asking God for a sign. She had looked out of the window and his car had driven past at a time of day when he was never normally in the area. Later she discovered that his boss had switched his schedule that morning and asked him to make an urgent delivery in the area near her home. Or again, he almost never went to the cinema, but he was shopping in a town about twenty miles away, decided on the spur of the moment to see a film and found her in there. It seemed obvious to them that these were encouragements from God as they prayed about whether it was his will for them to marry.

But it's dangerous to draw important conclusions from these coincidences. When you are in love and are not sure if the other person loves you, you think about every little word or gesture and sometimes read into them messages which were never intended. In the same way, when we want to know whether God is guiding us to separate or to remarry, it is all too easy to think he is giving us 'signs' and answers which are far from what he intends. Coincidences can confirm a decision reached for other clear reasons but should never be the determining factor which convinces us that a course of action is right.

There's an interesting example of this in the Old Testament when Abraham's servant was trying to find the woman whom God had chosen to be Isaac's wife (Genesis 24). The story begins when Abraham makes the servant swear a very solemn oath: 'I want you to swear by the Lord, the God of heaven and the God of earth, that you will not get a wife for my son from the daughters of the Canaanites, among whom I am living, but will go to my country and my own relatives and get a wife for my son Isaac' (vv. 3,4). This command to find a wife only among fellow Israelites and to abstain from intermarriage with surrounding nations was, of course, made out of loyalty to God and later formed part of God's command to all Israel (Deuteronomy 7:3-6). Abraham's servant journeyed back to Haran where his master had come from and his family still lived. He arrived at the well outside the town and didn't know how to begin his search. So he prayed that if he asked a woman for a drink and she then offered to draw water for his camels too, that would be the woman whom he had come for.

Precisely this happened. Rebekah arrived and not only agreed to draw water for the man but spontaneously offered to draw water also for his ten camels. This was surely a remarkable, and very rapid, answer to the servant's prayer; he might have been forgiven for deciding that this was a conclusive sign. But he didn't. As she drew the water for his camels, 'without saying a word, the man watched her closely to learn whether or not the Lord had made his journey successful' (Genesis 24:21). In other words, the 'sign' was not enough.

It was only when he asked her what family she was from and discovered that she was Abraham's near relative that he could exclaim, 'Praise be to the Lord, the God of my master Abraham, who has not abandoned his kindness and faithfulness to my master. As for me, the Lord has led me on the journey to the house of my master's relatives' (v. 27). He had been given a command by Abraham which was clearly in line with God's will for the marriage of his people. A sign was certainly an encouragement, but only obedience to the commands he had been given, both human and divine, convinced him that he had found the wife for Isaac.

The sign was important but could never have overridden the command. For the people of God under both old and new covenants, the command of God must be paramount. It is dangerous in the extreme if a supposed sign leads us to ignore what God has commanded.

The classic example of this comes in the story of Adam and Eve. God had clearly said, 'You must not eat from the tree of the knowledge of good and evil, for when you eat of it you will surely die' (Genesis 2:17). But then the woman, guided by the serpent, looked carefully at the tree and its fruit. The fruit was both 'good for food' and 'pleasing to the eye' (Genesis 3:6). Not only would it give pleasure, it was also 'desirable for gaining wisdom' (v. 6); and so she reasoned that there could be no harm in eating it and she ate, with disastrous consequences.

That story warns us never to look at our circumstances, draw conclusions from them and act on those conclusions rather than following the revealed command of God. We could easily find that we are playing into the hands of the devil (the serpent) rather than obeying God.

I've prayed a lot about it and feel at peace. Is that God guiding me?

Prayer is of course vital as we seek God's will about the great questions to do with our marriage, divorce and possible remarriage. It would be unthinkable to wrestle with these issues and not pray a great deal as we do so.

But inward peace as we pray is not a sure pointer to the will of God. We feel at peace when our conscience is untroubled, and certainly our consciences often reflect accurately the demands of God. But they are not an infallible guide. They can, for example, be influenced by false assumptions which owe more to the non-Christian world we live in than the Christian teaching which should now direct all our thinking and action. Paul calls this a 'weak conscience' in 1 Corinthians 8.

Or again, our consciences can be perverted and approve what is in fact against the will of God. Paul writes about people whose 'minds and consciences are corrupted. They claim to know God, but by their actions they deny him' (Titus 1:15,16).

This means that the peace we feel when we pray cannot be fully trusted to show us the will of God for our lives. Paul has this advice when we are disturbed about any issue: 'Do not be anxious about anything, but in everything, by prayer and petition, with thanksgiving, present your requests to God.' It is important to understand the promise that follows: 'And the peace of God, which transcends all understanding, will guard your hearts and minds in Christ Jesus' (Philippians 4:6,7). This is not a promise that when we pray about a thorny issue, we will know God's peace and that will be a clear indication of the action we should take. It is a promise that as we give over our anxieties to God in prayer and bring our requests to him, he will give us a peace that directs our whole being, including our thinking (our 'hearts and minds'), to Jesus Christ.

A true peace from God, then, doesn't bypass our listening to Christ's recorded teaching and obeying it. On the contrary, in the verses immediately following, Paul makes it abundantly clear that true peace can only come as we give careful attention to the teaching of Christ and his apostles, and obey it fully: 'Whatever you have learned or received or heard from me . . . put it into practice. And the God of peace will be with you' (Philippians 4:9).

Can I trust God with this decision?

When it comes to questions of marriage, singleness, single parenting, divorce and whether remarriage is or is not permitted to us as Christians, we find it hard to trust God. We fear that his way may be too demanding and that he may not have our best interests at heart. We fear that he may consign us to a life of loneliness and unhappiness.

The words of Proverbs 3:5-8 are very reassuring:

Trust in the Lord with all your heart and lean not on your own understanding;
in all your ways acknowledge him, and he will make your paths straight.
Do not be wise in your own eyes; fear the Lord and shun evil.
This will bring health to your body and nourishment to your bones.

These verses tell us something we must not do: 'Lean not on your own understanding . . . Do not be wise in your own eyes.' We often come to the Scriptures convinced that we know best what will be good for us, what will contribute to our happiness, our well-being, even our spiritual growth. We have reasoned it out and convinced ourselves. But Proverbs urges us to abandon that thinking which has worked it all out for ourselves with only a passing nod to what God has revealed.

Instead, we are to do three things. 'Trust in the Lord with all your heart' urges us to put all our confidence in God and his good purposes for our life. 'In all your ways acknowledge him' means that our decisions must be made, and our behaviour worked out, in dependence on him. 'Fear the Lord and shun evil' commands us not just to say that we hold God in awe but to show it by turning away from any thought or action that he forbids.

The promises are superb for those who will obey those three commands. 'The Lord will make your paths straight.' So much confusion and uncertainty often engulf those who have been through separation or divorce; we are paralysed, we haven't the confidence to take decisions. It is therefore an enormous relief that if we trust in the Lord, he will make our paths straight.

'This will bring health to your body and nourishment to your bones.' It may seem a strange promise, but in fact the trauma of separation often brings a breakdown of health. Any doctor knows that divorce, like bereavement, can have very distressing physical side-effects. And these are only exacerbated for Christians if we are struggling against what we really know is the will of God. That's why trusting him, and obeying him, often brings 'health to your body'.

God, and God alone, can be trusted with these big decisions.

Key verses

Jesus said, 'If anyone loves me, he will obey my teaching. My Father will love him, and we will come to him and make our home with him. He who does not love me will not obey my teaching. These words you hear are not my own; they belong to the Father who sent me' (John 14:23,24).

CHAPTER 3

QUESTIONS ABOUT MY (FIRST) MARRIAGE

David was visibly distressed as he talked with me coming back on a train from a conference. He and Michelle had married young; she had been just nineteen and her parents had tried to dissuade her from it. For the first four years everything seemed to be going well; they were making great plans to move house and then, in about eighteen months, to try for a family.

But gradually Michelle talked to him less and less; she didn't seem to care about him any longer. Then he discovered she was having an affair. He was hurt and very angry, there were stormy rows and in the end she left to live with the other man. It was at about this time, partly because of the support church members gave him, that David became a Christian.

After about eight months, Michelle's new relationship crumbled. She got in touch with David again, talked about moving back. But in the meantime he had got used to the idea that their marriage was over and had begun to be attracted to a Christian woman in the church. Now he was confused. What were his responsibilities? And in particular, how should he now view his marriage to Michelle?

What happened, from God's point of view, when I got married?

It's absolutely right to begin our thinking about divorce and remarriage with questions about marriage itself. In fact, it's where we must begin. Jesus made it quite clear that we will never understand his teaching about divorce until we have grasped what he teaches about marriage. That's why when he was asked a question about divorce, he refused to answer it until he had first explained what God does when we marry (Matthew 19:3-8; Mark 10:2-9).

In particular, Jesus says that two things happen when any couple marry. To make both points, he first quotes from the story in Genesis 2 of the creation of man and woman. This story not only describes how Adam met and formed a marriage relationship with Eve. In its conclusion, which is the climax of the story, it explains the nature of any and every human marriage: 'A man will leave his father and mother and be united to his wife, and they will become one flesh' (Genesis 2:24).

Jesus quotes this verse as his fundamental understanding of what happens when any man and any woman marry. He makes no comment on the leaving of parents, but deliberately concentrates on the other two parts of the statement, in each case drawing his own conclusion which lies at the heart of a Christian understanding of marriage.

First, says Jesus, *God joins the couple together.* Genesis 2 simply says that in marriage a man is 'united to his wife' and becomes 'one flesh'. But Jesus does not see any marriage as a purely human affair. Because God created the difference in the sexes (Matthew 19:4) and did so with a view to human marriage (v. 5), it is God who joins a couple together: 'Therefore what God has joined together', says Jesus, 'let man not separate' (Matthew 19:6; Mark 10:9). Jesus is not merely saying that God is in favour of marriage or that marriage was God's idea in the first place. He is saying that every couple who marry are joined together by God. Genesis

2:24 was talking about every marrying man ('For this reason a man.. . .'); Jesus is also talking about every marrying couple when he says that God joins them together.

Secondly, Jesus says that *the couple become one flesh*. Again he quotes Genesis 2:24 that in marriage 'The two ['a man' and 'his wife'] will become one flesh' (Matthew 19:5; Mark 10:8). Again he draws out from it what is implied but not stated: 'So they are no longer two, but one [literally: one flesh]' (Matthew 19:6; Mark 10:8).

This takes place at marriage. When Jesus, quoting Genesis 2:24, says, 'The two will become one flesh,' he does not mean that this will happen gradually during the course of their married life. Genesis 2:24 refers to what has consistently happened at every marriage since that of Adam and Eve. This is made clear by Christ's unequivocal statement: 'So they *are* no longer two, but one [my italics].'

Jesus denies something and he states something. He denies that the most fundamental truth about David and Michelle, or any couple after their marriage, is their separateness. Of course we remain individuals, but Jesus states that the essential truth about us if we are married, especially from God's perspective, is that we 'are no longer two'. Rather, we are 'one flesh'. This means, of course, far more than that we have had sexual intercourse. It means that from God's perspective the most significant fact about any husband and wife is that they are one. And this becomes the fundamental reality about them, says Jesus, at the moment when they are joined together by God in marriage.

What if we were married in a registry office?

People often imagine that while God may join together a couple who are married in church, this cannot be the case if the ceremony is purely secular in a registry office. This is based on the misunderstanding that for a couple to be married in the eyes of God there must have been some strongly religious element to their wedding and it must have taken place in a religious building or at least in the presence of a religious official. In fact, Israelite and Jewish marriage could be very simple and normally took place in the home or tent, not at the shrine, temple or synagogue. When Isaac married Rebekah, it is described in the simplest terms: 'Then Isaac brought her into his mother Sarah's tent. He took Rebekah, and she became his wife; and he loved her. So Isaac was comforted after his mother's death' (Genesis 24:67, NRSV).

There is no specifically religious ceremony. Rather, he 'brought her' in a simple but deliberate and almost certainly public way into his family's tent; he 'took' her, which may mean that he entered into a marriage agreement ('covenant', see Malachi 2:14) with her or may mean that he had intercourse with her; and in this way 'she became his wife'.

Certainly the sexual consummation of the marriage was important. Laban brings his daughter to Jacob on the day of the marriage feast so that he can sleep with her (Genesis 29:23); and in the Apocryphal book of Tobit, the Jewish mother first makes the bridal room ready and leads her daughter, the bride, into it, and then the family or guests escort the bridegroom to her (Tobit 7:16–8:1).

But no religious ceremony was necessary; and yet Jesus stated that such couples – indeed, every married couple – are joined together by God.

What if we weren't Christians at the time?

Or what if I wasn't? Or my husband/wife wasn't? Can it really be said that God joins together even those who don't believe in him?

This seems to have been a problem for several Christians at Corinth. They wrote to Paul with a number of sexual and marital questions. They weren't at all sure that sex had any place in the Christian life, and the sentence in 1 Corinthians 7:1, 'It is well for a man not to touch a woman' (RSV), may well have been a quotation from their letter, expressing their views.

One of the results of this view seems to have been their conviction that if a couple married and one partner subsequently became a Christian, the Christian should repudiate the marriage because it had not been made 'in the Lord' (a phrase used of Christian marriage in 1 Corinthians 7:39, RSV).

Paul vigorously denies this (1 Corinthians 7:12-16). What Jesus had said about marriage in general – that a couple should stay together and not separate (vv. 10,11) – was just as true for a marriage where one partner is a Christian and the other is not. In this situation also the Christian partner is to take no initiative in ending the marriage, nor to think of his marriage as in any way less valid or real in God's eyes (vv. 12,13). Of course he will want to see the non-Christian partner converted (v. 16), but if the non-Christian remains stubbornly opposed to the Christian faith, that gives the Christian no grounds for considering himself anything other than married. It is only if the non-Christian insists on a divorce that the Christian is not duty-bound to refuse it and fight it (v. 15). Our conversion, then, has no effect on whether or not God sees us as married.

This is also implied by Christ's teaching on marriage. When he wants to explain what God does at marriage, he appeals over the head of Moses (who gave the law to Israel) and even goes beyond Abraham (the first 'father' of Israel) to what he twice calls 'the beginning' (Matthew 19:4,8), the creation of the original man and woman from whom all humanity springs. As we have already seen, Genesis 2:24, which Jesus quotes, draws conclusions from this original marriage for the marriage of every man and woman. Marriage is marriage; God joins the couple together, however much or little they are aware of him.

Was I, in God's eyes, married to people I've lived with?

Almost all young people today in Western Europe and North

America are sexually experienced before they marry. In a survey called *Young Britain*, carried out among eighteen to thirty-four year olds in 1990, 96% condoned or approved unmarried couples living together. The Government Office of Population Censuses and Surveys reported 819,000 recorded conceptions in 1993, of which 44% were conceived outside marriage.

So if sexual union is an important element in marriage, does that mean that in God's eyes I am married to the first person I slept with? No, because while there can be no full marriage without sexual consummation, sexual intercourse alone does not constitute marriage. There must also be a desire for, and formal consent to, marriage.

This is clear from both Old and New Testaments. Under the Mosaic law, a man who had slept with an unmarried woman was obliged to offer to marry her. However, her family might refuse this arrangement. The man would then make financial amends for what he had done to the woman but he was not considered to have married her (Exodus 22:16,17).

In the Corinthian church, while some Christians (as we have seen) thought that all sex should be avoided, others were visiting prostitutes. Paul acknowledges that the sexual act can never be completely casual; even with a prostitute it creates a bond between the man and the woman. Paul goes so far as to quote: 'The two will become one flesh.' However, it is quite clear that he does not mean that a true marriage has taken place because he tells the Christians to 'flee from' their sexual immorality whereas he is just about to tell married couples to remain together (1 Corinthians 6:15-20; 7:10,11).

Sexual intercourse does not create marriage, therefore. You cannot be married to someone merely by sleeping with them or even living with them. You cannot go to bed with someone for one night – or even every night for many years – and wake up to discover that you are married.

Marriage is a definite and conscious act. It is also a public act, involving other people. The marriage ceremony may be very simple, but you are only married to someone when you have publicly consented to marry them in accordance with the laws of the land where you live (Jewish marriage customs varied at different times, and Jesus accepted Greeks and Romans as being married).

What if I wasn't ready for marriage?

What if I married too young, like David and Michelle? What if I didn't really know what I was doing? Or if I got married for the wrong reasons: to get away from home, or because I was pregnant?

There are many reasons why couples get married: some good and some not so good. In fact, most of us get married for a whole variety of rather mixed reasons. For a man to offer to marry a woman, for example, because he has made her pregnant is not a dishonourable reason to marry. Under the old covenant, he had to make this offer if he had slept with a woman because he had dishonoured her and robbed her of her virginity (Exodus 22:16,17; compare Deuteronomy 22:28,29). In fact, most Western nations until comparatively recently, and the majority of nations still today, would consider it obviously right for a man who made a woman pregnant to marry her. There are good reasons for this: a child needs not just a man and a woman in order to be secure and develop healthily; every child needs the closest possible relationship with his father and his mother.

Again, it may be true that it is often preferable to marry in one's mid to late twenties, or later still. But that doesn't mean that those who marry young, perhaps while still in their teens, are not married. It may be appropriate for society to set a minimum legal age for marriage, but beyond that it cannot be said that a marriage is invalid because it was contracted young.

The fact is that none of us fully know what we are doing when we get married. As a clergyman, I talk with a large number of engaged couples. Almost all of them are convinced that they are ideally suited to one another, that they have come to terms with any differences and that they will meet no problem which they can't surmount comparatively easily.

In practice, marriage is a surprise to us all. In some ways it can prove better than we anticipated, in many ways it will be different and, for most couples, it will in many ways be much harder, more complex and more full of difficulties. But none of these things mean that our marriage didn't take place or that God didn't join us together.

What if I realised it was a mistake even before we got married?

It is common to have cold feet about a forthcoming marriage, especially during what is often the very pressurised period of engagement. In some people these doubts are strong, particularly if we discover new and disturbing aspects of our fiancé(e)'s character or past history of which we were unaware before. As (now married) we look back, we can see that we should have taken those misgivings more seriously and not listened to the reassuring advice that our family or friends may have given.

Nevertheless, we went through with the wedding and made the marriage vows. Under the law of the land, we are treated as responsible people who have voluntarily taken on duties and responsibilities, and we are then held to them. In the nineteenth century, Lord Stowell made a statement about the law which still stands: 'The parties are concluded to mean seriously and deliberately and intentionally what they have avowed in the presence of God and man.'

The Bible also treats us in the same way as responsible men and women: 'When you make a vow to God, do not delay in fulfilling it. . . . It is better not to vow than to make a vow and not fulfil it. . . . Do not protest to the temple messenger, "My vow was a mistake." Why should God be angry at what you say and destroy the work of your hands? Much dreaming and many

words are meaningless. Therefore stand in awe of God'
(Ecclesiastes 5:4-7).

The teaching here is straightforward. When we make a vow,
even if we subsequently realise it was a mistake, God holds us to
it. Before making the vow was the time to review whether it
should be made. Once it has been made, it is to be fulfilled.

What if I never really loved my partner?

In our Western culture we marry for love. That was also quite
common in the biblical world. 'Jacob was in love with Rachel
and said [to her father], "I'll work for you seven years in return
for your younger daughter Rachel." . . . So Jacob served seven
years to get Rachel, but they seemed like only a few days to him
because of his love for her' (Genesis 29:18,20).

Samson's relationship with Delilah began in the same way:
'He fell in love with a woman in the Valley of Sorek whose name
was Delilah' (Judges 16:4). But later she complains to him that
his love cannot be genuine as he won't talk to her and tell her
what's on his mind: 'How can you say "I love you" when you
won't confide in me?' (Judges 6:15).

But love can turn to hatred. Amnon's relationship with Tamar
began with love: 'Amnon, son of David, fell in love with Tamar
the beautiful sister of Absalom' (2 Samuel 13:1). But after he
had violated her sexually, 'then Amnon hated her with intense
hatred. In fact, he hated more than he had loved her. Amnon
said to her, "Get up and get out!"' (2 Samuel 13:15).

It can be that way in a modern marriage. Love can turn to
frustration, irritation, anger and hatred. We may want to say:
'Get up and get out!'; or to get out of this hell ourselves. We can
question whether we ever really loved our marriage partner or
just imagined that we were in love. Especially (though not only)
if we find ourselves falling in love with someone else and
experiencing feelings we have never known within marriage.
This at last is the real thing. This is love.

But nowhere in the Bible does it say that being in love is essential to marriage. The Bible never even hints that if we are not in love we are not truly married, or that if we were never in love there was never a marriage in the first place.

It is true that the Bible expects marriage partners to love one another. The New Testament repeatedly tells husbands, in particular, to love their wives (Ephesians 5:25,28,33; Colossians 3:19). But this is not the Greek word *erō/erōs*, romantic or sexual love, from which we get our word erotic. This is *agapaō/agapē*, which mirrors Christ's love for us.

It is explicitly committed, self-sacrificing love. In his classic passage on marriage, Paul says: 'Husbands, love your wives just as Christ loved the church *and gave himself up for her* . . . Husbands ought to love their wives as their own bodies' (Ephesians 5:25,28). A married Christian has to learn – especially if (s)he is in a marriage which gives her no pleasure and where there never was much, if any, love – that marriage is not primarily about being in love but about giving and giving and giving again to our marriage partner, even when our efforts are neither appreciated nor even recognised.

When we married, we promised 'to have and to hold, from this day forward, for better for worse'; that means whether our love for our marriage partner is strong or is non-existent.

What about the idea of nullity?

In view of Christ's teaching about divorce (which we shall look at in later chapters), Christians have understandably been wary about initiating divorce proceedings. But can a marriage be declared null? Is it possible to look back on a wedding and say that it was invalid?

Two of the essential ingredients to any valid marriage are consent and consummation. The man and the woman must voluntarily enter into the marriage and must publicly give their *consent.* Even in early biblical times, with arranged marriages, the consent of both parties was normally, perhaps always, required. So, when Abraham sends his servant to Haran to find a wife for Isaac from 'my country and my own relatives', the servant replies, 'What if the woman is unwilling to come back with me to this land?' And Abraham answers, 'If the woman is unwilling to come back with you, then you will be released from this oath of mine' (Genesis 24:5,8).

In the event, the family wants ten days to get ready and say goodbye to Rebekah, whereas Abraham's servant would like to get going with her immediately. The family replies: '"Let's call the girl and ask her about it." So they called Rebekah and asked her, "Will you go with this man?" "I will go," she said' (vv. 55-58).

It is for this reason that in the wedding service, the first question asked is: 'Will you have (or take) this woman/man to be your wife/husband?' and each party has to respond separately: 'I will.' This is known as the Declaration of Consent.

It is possible to imagine situations when that consent was only given under intolerable pressure: for example, if a bride's parents had withdrawn food from her, or said that she could under no circumstance leave the home until she agreed to marry. But it would have to be extreme pressure so that the voluntary nature of the public consent was almost totally obliterated. Under these circumstances a marriage might be declared null. It would not be sufficient if friends and family were urging on a woman (or man) despite her hesitations, and she was persuaded by their pressure and gave her consent, though she could in fact have refused it. I deliberately used the phrase '*intolerable* pressure' in the first sentence of this paragraph.

Wilful failure to *consummate* a marriage would also be a reason for declaring it null. Sexual intercourse may subsequently be refused and the marriage still remain in existence, but an initial sexual act is necessary (unless it is physically impossible) to 'consummate' the marriage and bring it fully into being. A friend of mine is a US citizen who technically married an immigrant in order to bring her into the country. There was no sexual union and no intention of having sex and some years later the marriage was rightly declared null.

One further reason for declaring a marriage null might be one partner's lying about some significant event which happened before the marriage and which, had it been known, might have prevented the other from marrying him/her. In Old Testament times it was assumed that both partners were sexual virgins at marriage; a cloth was laid underneath the couple to gather the blood from the ruptured hymen of the bride. This proved that the bride had been a sexual virgin. If no such proof was shown and it became apparent that she had already had sexual experience, then under the Mosaic law she was to be put to death (see Deuteronomy 22:13-21).

We obviously live in a society where we make very different assumptions about the state of a person's sexual experience before marriage and where the penalties for misdemeanour are different. Nevertheless, if one partner deliberately hid a vital fact about his premarital life which might have caused the other partner to refuse marriage (for example, that he was the father of children by another woman), then this could be grounds for declaring the marriage void.

But great care must be taken here. This cannot apply to lies or deceptions *after* marriage, because marriage is a deliberate leap into the unknown, whatever the future may bring; we take each other 'for better, for worse . . .'. It is also essential that it should not be the partners themselves, or one of them, who declare the marriage null. They are interested parties and their judgement may well be clouded. It must be some external body – judges or acknowledged church leaders – who declare marriages null.

Some Christians believe that marriages can be declared null because of psychological immaturity and unpreparedness for married life at the time of the wedding. But the vast majority of churches have rightly rejected this approach. None of us fully know what marriage will involve until we are married; none of us are fully psychologically mature and, in fact, marriage is often a means by which we grow in maturity; and if we waited until we were fully prepared for marriage, we would never marry.

There are, then, rare occasions on which a marriage can and should be declared null. But they are very few and far between. A couple who agreed to get married and have had sexual intercourse will almost never be candidates for having their marriage nullified.

What if I find it hard to believe that God ever 'joined us together'?

This is an understandable reaction, especially if you and/or your partner were not Christians when you married, if you deliberately chose not to get married in church and preferred a registry office, and particularly if you and your partner have had frequent rows or icy months of non-communication and the reality of your marriage is so horribly different from what you had anticipated.

When you presented yourselves before the registrar (or Christian minister), he or she treated you as responsible human beings. Providing you were free to marry in the eyes of the law, he or she married you.

God treats us in exactly the same way. His will is that most (not all) human beings should get married. Marriage, which according to Genesis 2 was God's idea in the first place, is not confined to those who believe in him and belong to God's people. It is for non-Christians as well as Christians, atheist as well as believer ('for this reason a man. . .' [Genesis 2:24, quoted by Jesus in Mark 10:7; Matthew 19:5]).

God is present at every marriage. Behind the registrar or the minister stands God, whether he is recognised as being present or not. In almost all cultures, witnesses are required at a wedding. God is a witness, the most important witness, at every wedding. Thus, when Malachi castigates Israelite husbands for their unfaithfulness in marriage, he can say, 'The Lord is acting as the witness between you and the wife of your youth [a reference to the original wedding], because you have broken faith with her, though she is your partner, the wife of your marriage covenant' (Malachi 2:14).

But there is an even more significant factor. God is not only the witness, he is the celebrant at every wedding. He is the real registrar, the real minister, again whether he is acknowledged or not. In every marriage, as Jesus says, 'God has joined [the couple] together' (Mark 10:9; Matthew 19:6).

If the marriage has broken down, are we really still 'one flesh'?

It seems to many couples a mockery to say that they are 'one flesh' when sexual relations may have ceased years ago, love has turned to hatred, the partners cannot bear being in the same room as each other and have perhaps lived apart for months or years.

But when the Bible says that a couple are 'one flesh', it is not a statement about psychological or emotional oneness. Of course psychological oneness is important in a healthy marriage. Of course it is important that a married couple should feel at one, should communicate well, should share each other's thoughts and emotions as well as bodies. This psychological oneness is something which can grow in a well-functioning marriage and be destroyed in a dysfunctional one.

It is not this which the Bible is describing when it says a couple at marriage 'become one flesh'. Rather, this is a statement about their essential relationship. In Christ's eyes, the most fundamental fact about them is that, from the moment of their marriage, 'they are no longer two, but one' (Mark 10:8; Matthew 19:6). This remains the bedrock fact about their relationship, even if it is far from how they are living out their lives in practice. It is how God sees them. It is how Christ urges them to see themselves. It is how Christ urges their family and friends to see them (Mark 10:8,9; Matthew 19:5,6).

How should I view my first marriage?

As still existing. When a marriage is very painful and we are
screaming with its pain, we want to think that it is dead and
gone so that we can leave it behind completely. When we have
been separated or divorced for some time and we long for relief
from the constant opening of wounds, we would like to think
that there is nothing left of the marriage.

Of course it is important, if your partner has left for good, to
face up to that gradually and build a new life around that hard
reality. But it simply isn't true that a marriage is ever dead and
buried while the separated or divorced partner is still alive.

This is true at the psychological level. Often contacts between
the marriage partners have to be maintained: over children, over
financial arrangements, over weddings, funerals or other family
occasions. Even when that is not necessary, there are frequent
reminders of one's partner: through mutual friends, or in
familiar places or situations which remind you of him/her, or
seeing someone in a shop or across the street who walks like
your partner or laughs like him. The song goes: 'I'm gonna wash
that man right out of my hair', but it's very much easier to say
than to do.

It is also true that the marriage continues to be alive at the
level of essential reality. You remain, at the deepest level, one
flesh with your partner. The marriage bond is still in place. It is
finally destroyed when 'death us do part' (1 Corinthians 7:39;
Romans 7:2,3), but until then, whether we like it or not, it
exists.

Is there any hope for my marriage?

Yes, there is. Jesus taught that marriage was God's idea in the
first place (Matthew 19:4,5). And what God has planned, he
will support. Jesus taught that God joins each couple together
when they marry (vv. 5,6), that he has joined you together with

your wife or husband. And since he has joined you together, he will certainly give you the resources to stay together or to come back together, however long and hard the road.

In fact, a major part of the work God has given Jesus is to support those who feel desperate and to turn their pain into joy. This is how the Messiah speaks in the prophecy of Isaiah: 'The Spirit of the Sovereign Lord is on me, because the Lord has anointed me to preach good news to the poor. He has sent me to bind up the broken-hearted, to proclaim freedom for the captives . . . to comfort all who mourn, and provide for those who grieve in Zion – to bestow on them a crown of beauty instead of ashes, the oil of gladness instead of mourning, and a garment of praise instead of a spirit of despair' (Isaiah 61:1-3).

These are words which Jesus applied to himself (Luke 4:16-21), but they met with unbelief in his hearers and so did them no good (Luke 4:22-29; compare Mark 6:1-6; Matthew 13:54-58). We must not make their mistake again. We need to believe that Christ can meet us in our despair and change us. Many deeply troubled marriages have been given fresh beauty from what seemed like ashes.

Indeed, hope is one of the great hallmarks both of God himself and of those who trust him through the darkest times. That is why Paul can say, 'May the God of hope fill you with all joy and peace as you trust in him, so that you may overflow with hope by the power of the Holy Spirit' (Romans 15:13).

Key verse

Jesus taught: 'The Creator . . . said, "For this reason a man will leave his father and mother and be united to his wife, and the two will become one flesh". So they are no longer two, but one' (Matthew 19:4-6).

CHAPTER 4

QUESTIONS ABOUT SEPARATION/DIVORCE

Hazel's life had become unbearable. It was at least nine months since she and Sean had had a proper conversation. For the most part, communication was restricted to: 'What's for supper?' and 'I need a clean shirt for tomorrow'. Recently, he had taken to being away without explanation for two or three nights at a time. He would come back smelling heavily of drink, but she told me she was almost certain he wasn't having an affair.

Hazel looked haggard. She didn't know how much longer she could cope.

When can it be right for a Christian to separate?

This was the question Hazel asked me. She felt she had been pushed almost to breaking point and she wanted to know, as a Christian, whether she had the right to leave Sean. Many others have asked the same question. But however you ask it – whether because you're in the midst of a very painful marriage or because you are thinking more dispassionately about a Christian understanding of divorce – it's the wrong place to begin.

In most wedding services, Christ's words are quoted: 'What God has joined together, let man not separate' (Mark 10:9;

Matthew 19:6). In the Anglican service, this comes as a high point in the service, immediately after the declaration that the couple are now husband and wife. And it is Jesus' basic answer to the question: 'Is it lawful for a man to divorce his wife?' (Mark 10:2).

This, then, has to be our basic attitude as Christians to divorce. We cannot primarily ask questions about when it is right to separate because our fundamental conviction is that God joins every married couple together and it is not for anyone – the couple themselves or any third person – to try to undo, or even weaken, what God has done.

Happily, this conviction is widespread among Christians; we know that Christ spoke strongly against divorce. As a result, Christians have been much less ready than their secular contemporaries to reach for divorce as a solution to their marital problems. I have no national statistics for divorce among Christians, and of course it is true that Christians are influenced by trends in society and are divorcing more now than they did fifteen or twenty-five years ago. Nevertheless, it is my consistent experience that the divorce rate among Christians is considerably lower than in the community around us.

Christians who have battled to keep going in a painful and empty marriage are often grateful in the long run that they have heeded Christ's teaching and held on to what had seemed for a long time like an unbearably difficult relationship. A few months ago I talked with a man very seriously considering leaving his wife. He thought and read a lot and, having decided to keep going in the marriage, wrote to me: 'Last year has been more painful than ever, but I think having this crisis has helped. I certainly came to the end of my own and other "man-made" resources. I feel a lot better now; *not* optimistic but emotionally sounder and more at peace.'

Yet Hazel's question cannot be ducked. Granted that a Christian's attitude must be that divorce is in all but exceptional cases not an option, are there any circumstances in which divorce is permissible? Jesus gives one and one only: sexual unfaithfulness. 'I tell you that anyone who divorces his wife, except for marital unfaithfulness, and marries another woman commits adultery' (Matthew 19:9); 'I tell you that anyone who divorces his wife, except for marital unfaithfulness, causes her to become an adulteress' (Matthew 5:32). This is the only reason given by Christ in the Gospels which can justify divorce.

What kind of sexual unfaithfulness makes it permissible to divorce?

So what does this 'marital unfaithfulness' mean? In both cases the Greek word is *porneia,* a very general word which the standard dictionary of New Testament Greek defines as covering 'every kind of unlawful sexual intercourse'.[4] Clearly its principal meaning here is adultery, that is: heterosexual intercourse with someone other than your marriage partner; but it will also include homosexual practice and incest.

But it is important to stress that in these cases divorce is *permitted* to the offended partner; it is not made inevitable. It is probably significant in Matthew's Gospel that when the Pharisees asked: "Why then . . . did Moses *command* that a man give his wife a certificate of divorce?" Jesus replied, "Moses *permitted* you to divorce your wives . . ." (Matthew 19:7,8, my italics). Even Moses only allowed divorce; and of course the circumstances under which Jesus will permit divorce are a great deal more restricted (v. 9). But neither Moses nor Jesus insisted on divorce in any circumstance.

In this, as in so many other ways, Jesus was different from his contemporaries. Roman law obliged a husband to divorce his adulterous wife; Jewish law had the same requirement: the Mosaic law's punishment of death for adultery (e.g. Leviticus 20:10) had by now almost entirely been replaced by divorce (e.g. Matthew 1:18,19). But Jesus does not demand divorce in any circumstance; he merely permits it when one partner has been sexually unfaithful.

This is a vital distinction. Sexual infidelity is widespread today. It is reckoned that six out of ten wives are at some stage unfaithful to their husbands, and seven out of ten husbands are unfaithful to their wives. But adultery does not of itself 'destroy' the marriage; it does not break the marriage bond. It certainly brings the marriage, in almost all cases, under enormous stress. It does permit the offended Christian to divorce his/her partner. It betrays the marriage, it undermines the marriage, but it does not automatically destroy the marriage.

The fact is that many married couples, whether Christians or where neither partner is a Christian, have faced up to sexual infidelity in one or both partners, confessed, forgiven and been able to carry on in a committed marriage relationship, often (perhaps after a shaky time) emerging the stronger for the honesty and forgiveness between them. It is almost always a mistake to respond immediately to the news of sexual unfaithfulness with an outraged: 'That's it. It's all over now', even if the unfaithfulness is not for the first time.

What if my partner is not a Christian?

Paul writes about a situation not mentioned by Jesus in his teaching on divorce: the case of a mixed marriage where one partner is a Christian and the other is not (1 Corinthians 7:12-16). It has often been said that the New Testament gives two grounds for divorce: adultery (mentioned by Jesus in the Gospels) and desertion by an unbeliever (mentioned by Paul in 1 Corinthians).

In fact, this is not the case. If anything, this represents the position of some Corinthian Christians who almost certainly raised the matter in their letter (7:1). They seem to have believed that in general: 'It is well for a man not to touch a woman' (7:1, RSV; probably – in view of Paul's disagreement with this blanket statement – a quotation of the Corinthians' opinion which Paul found expressed in their letter). With this understanding, it was natural for them to think that a Christian was defiled by contact with a non-Christian marriage partner (e.g. v. 14) and should divorce him/her.

Paul will have none of this. He first specifically quotes Christ's teaching, saying that divorce is not to be thought of by any Christian (vv. 10,11). He then turns from the general principle to the specific situation of the so-called 'mixed marriage'. His verdict is precisely the same as Christ's: there is to be no divorce. 'If any brother has a wife who is not a believer and she is willing to live with him, he must not divorce her. And if a woman has a husband who is not a believer and he is willing to live with her, she must not divorce him' (vv. 12,13).

It is only if the non-Christian partner positively insists on leaving that the Christian can agree to a divorce and need not feel duty-bound to obstruct it: 'But if the unbeliever leaves, let him do so. A believing man or woman is not bound in such circumstances; God has called us to live in peace' (v. 15). But this is quite unlike the case where a partner has been unfaithful. It is not a new ground for divorce; it is merely a reason for accepting a divorce which the other partner initiates and not being duty-bound to fight it.

It is often assumed that because both Old and New Testaments forbid marriages between believers and unbelievers (e.g. Deuteronomy 7:3,4; 1 Corinthians 7:39; 2 Corinthians 6:14-18), the situation envisaged here must be where a couple have married as non-Christians and one partner has subsequently been converted. This may indeed have been the kind of situation which Paul had principally in mind, but there is nothing in the context to restrict his teaching to that kind of mixed marriage; it applies just as much to couples where a Christian, against the biblical commands, marries a non-Christian. If so, it is a further example of the fact that we may have made a mistake in marrying this particular person, but having entered the marriage, made our vows and been joined together by God, we are to stick in there.

What if my partner abuses me or my children?

What if my partner has sexually abused me or my children? Or if he has been violent towards us?

Clearly we must protect our children from sexual abuse. This is most certainly included in the *porneia* (sexual sin) which Jesus says is an absolutely valid ground for divorce.

It is harder to assess sexual abuse of the marriage partner. Paul says that in marriage a husband gives control over his body to his wife and a wife gives control over her body to her husband: 'The wife does not rule over her own body, but the husband does; likewise the husband does not rule over his own body, but the wife does' (1 Corinthians 7:4, RSV). In the Church of England's wedding service, this is expressed with the words: 'With my body I honour you. All that I am I give to you, and all that I have I share with you.' Paul draws the conclusion in sexual matters: 'Do not deprive each other except by mutual consent and for a time' (v. 5). These verses call for mutual respect in sexual practice: sometimes it will mean abstaining from sex for the sake of one's partner, but the emphasis is on agreeing to sex, even when you are not feeling like it.

But what if one partner forces sex on the other (some call this 'marital rape'), or insists on sexual practices that the other finds repugnant? Certainly these things go beyond Paul's command that in the sexual realm 'the husband should fulfil his marital duty to his wife, and likewise the wife to her husband' (v. 3). But they would not under any normal circumstances be adequate grounds for divorce. Only if the husband (it would normally be the man) consistently and with threats insisted on positively degrading practices, which any Christian would consider abhorrent even between consenting partners, might this perhaps come under *porneia* and be sufficient grounds for divorce.

Violence is a different matter again. Almost all Christian authors agree that when there is real danger to yourself or your children, it is permissible to separate from your partner. It cannot be right to put up with being hit or thrown down the stairs time and time again. But we need to be careful here. The New Testament mentions *porneia* alone as a legitimate ground for divorce. While it is almost certainly right to see divorce as the lesser of two evils when there is persistent violence, we must be careful not to go on extending the moral right to divorce by adding more and more exceptions. It is absolutely clear that the whole thrust of Jesus' teaching is *against* divorce. Mark's Gospel makes no exception to this rule; Matthew mentions only one (marital unfaithfulness).

What if we've had no sex life for a long time?

This book has repeatedly stated that sex is part of marriage. Without the initial sexual consummation the marriage is not complete and can, in any normal situation, be declared null. Paul makes it absolutely clear that regular sexual intercourse is part of what we owe one another in marriage, whether we like the idea or not (1 Corinthians 7:3-5). In our vows, we specifically promise our bodies to one another.

But what if these promises are not fulfilled? It is natural to feel cheated if my partner refuses me sex. I married at least partly for sexual pleasure; I feel that she (or he) is cheating me of my right, that she is not keeping the promises she made to me. As Christians, we are not permitted to find sexual satisfaction elsewhere. So is this a further legitimate ground for divorce?

The answer to this must be: no. The New Testament frequently groups together instructions for husbands and wives, parents and children, employers and employees. Each of these lays out not their rights (the typical emphasis of the late twentieth century) but their duties and responsibilities (Ephesians 5:22–6:9; Colossians 3:18–4:1; 1 Peter 2:18–3:7).

The question naturally arises: if one party fails to fulfil their responsibilities, does this let the other party off the hook? This issue is specifically addressed by the New Testament in the field of work. It is worth quoting at length because it has obvious implications for other relationships:

> Slaves, submit yourselves to your masters with all respect, not only to those who are good and considerate, but also to those who are harsh. For it is commendable if a man bears up under the pain of unjust suffering because he is conscious of God. . . . If you suffer for doing good and you endure it, this is commendable before God. To this you were called, because Christ suffered for you, leaving you an example, that you should follow in his steps. 'He committed no sin, and no deceit was found in his mouth' [Isaiah 53:9]. When they hurled their insults at him, he did not retaliate; when he suffered, he made no threats. Instead, he entrusted himself to him who judges justly. (1 Peter 2:18-23).

Peter goes on immediately to write about wives and husbands (1 Peter 3:1-7). The implication is obvious. If the wife fails in her marital responsibilities, for instance by refusing sex to her husband, or if the husband fails in his duties, for instance by failing to 'be considerate' and to 'treat [her] with respect' (3:7), then the aggrieved partner should still remain faithful and fulfil his or her marital duties. Of course they must seek to talk and work through their difficulties; certainly there will, as in the field of work, be suffering – unjust suffering which mirrors Christ's own – but these are not grounds for getting out of the relationship or even for withdrawing into a protective shell.

Nevertheless, sexual problems in marriage need to be taken seriously. It will very likely be wise to seek out confidential counsel, perhaps from your nearest Relate office, or by asking your GP to refer you to someone with psycho-sexual expertise. It is, of course, better to go as a couple but perfectly possible to seek help on your own. And as with so many problems in marriage, it is better to ask for help earlier rather than later when ingrained habits are harder (though not impossible) to work on.

What if life has become unbearable living together?

From 1969 until the late 1990s 'irretrievable breakdown' in marriage was the sole legitimate grounds, in the eyes of English law, for divorce. Adultery certainly remained one way of demonstrating that the marriage had broken down, but intolerable 'behaviour' became the most commonly cited evidence. Should Christians also widen the grounds for permissible divorce and say that it is morally acceptable to divorce when one partner (or both) have found it unbearable to live together?

We must come back to the teaching of Christ. He was asked a question about whether it was permissible to divorce (Mark 10:2). His answer was clear: God had created people as male and female with a view to marriage, they become one flesh in marriage. 'Therefore what God has joined together, let man not separate' (Mark 10:6-9; Matthew 19:4-6).

This understanding of marriage is reflected in the marriage vows. A couple promise each other 'to have and to hold, from this day forward, for better for worse . . . to love and to cherish, till death us do part'. Here is a specific promise to stick together when things are good and when they are extremely difficult, in joy and in deep suffering, when the marriage is a pleasure and when it has become 'unbearable'.

Jesus did of course give one exception, allowing a partner to break his/her vows and to initiate divorce. That exception is sexual unfaithfulness, and it is very specifically the only exception that he allows.

This is not a light issue. Precisely because marriage is the closest human relationship, it can bring unremitting, acute suffering which threatens to submerge us. But Christians are not left alone, to fend for themselves, in their suffering. Paul never belittled human pain, but he spoke from wide experience when he said, 'We also rejoice in our sufferings, because we know that suffering produces perseverance; perseverance, character; and character, hope. And hope does not disappoint us, because God has poured out his love into our hearts by the Holy Spirit, whom he has given us' (Romans 5:4,5). Many Christians have proved this true in what, without it, would be a genuinely intolerable marriage. They have not only matured as individuals but have known God's love for them to a depth that would have been impossible without their suffering.

Didn't Christ say 'no divorce' to protect first-century women?

Jewish wives in the first century could be dumped at will. Their husbands might be in a bad mood, or have a sudden whim, and summarily divorce them. Women were also not easily in a position to lead independent lives. So some Christians argue that it was to protect the wives of his day that Jesus gave this stern teaching against divorce. Now, of course, times have changed. In particular, women are much more often able to lead independent lives. So if Jesus were living in the West today, he would have a very different attitude to divorce.

What are we to make of this argument? It is certainly true that Jesus cared for the disadvantaged, especially those who were not able to stand up for themselves. It is also true that Jesus showed a respect and care for women which was far from typical of Jewish men in his day. It is, further, true that it was extraordinarily easy for Jewish husbands to divorce their wives, though in practice they availed themselves of this opportunity far less frequently than couples in the West do today.

However, there is no evidence whatsoever that it was because of social conditions in his day that Jesus forbade divorce. It would be much easier to argue this for Moses and the legislation that he introduced. In the Old Testament law on which the Jews based their practice of divorce, it is mentioned that a husband must give his wife 'a certificate of divorce' (Deuteronomy 24:1,3). This almost certainly was to protect the interests of the woman: so that she was not left in marital limbo (deserted but not divorced) and so that, in the old covenant context, she was free to remarry.

Jesus specifically says that this legislation was 'because your hearts were hard' (Mark 10:5; Matthew 19:8). It was not God's original intention and in the kingdom of God (i.e. under the new covenant) the permission to divorce was rescinded. It therefore was a response to cultural and spiritual conditions of Moses' day.

But Jesus' own teaching is not tied to the culture of his day. On the contrary, he explicitly refers it back to 'the beginning', to what had been 'the Creator's' purpose all along (Matthew 19:4-8). Christ's teaching on marriage and divorce stems from a creation ordinance which is valid for all peoples of all cultures and all times. The Christian, in particular, has no right to disregard it and no mandate to explain it away as irrelevant in the culture of our day.

Can a marriage 'die'?

On several occasions people have said to me, 'Our marriage died a long time ago'; 'My marriage has already long since ceased in all but name.' Is that an accurate way of speaking, so that a divorce is only the official burial of what has long since died?

Of course much that should be an essential part of marriage can die. All pleasure in the marriage can die. (Almost) all benefit to either party can die. Any sense of companionship can die and what is left can turn into bitter antagonism.

But the marriage relationship itself cannot die. At the point of marriage, God joins the couple together and they become one flesh. Jesus comments: 'So they are no longer two, but one' (Mark 10:8; Matthew 19:6). Only physical death, not the withdrawal of all that has been promised, can bring the marriage to an end. The marriage can go sour, it can bring far more pain than pleasure; but only death breaks the marriage bond: 'A woman is bound to her husband as long as he lives'

(1 Corinthians 7:39; compare Romans 7:2). Paul makes it quite clear that a man is in no different position.

Marriage really is 'till death us do part', until the physical death of one of the partners brings it to an end. That is a hard truth for many to accept, but to kick against it normally brings still greater pain to all those who are affected by a marriage break-up and to one or both of the couple themselves.

Is there a difference in God's eyes between separation and divorce?

Christians are well aware that divorce has been forbidden by Christ; it has only been permitted (not commanded) in the case of sexual unfaithfulness. But if it is forbidden to divorce, is it permissible to separate? Is there a distinction in God's eyes between separation and divorce?

Some people who want to argue for this distinction point to 1 Corinthians 7:10,11 where a wife is instructed not to 'separate from her husband' while a husband is told not to 'divorce his wife'. But in fact the two words are used interchangeably. In verse 13 the woman is told: 'she must not divorce [her husband]', and in verse 15 the word for 'separate' (NIV: 'leaves') is used of both sexes.

It is not even certain that Paul and his contemporaries would have understood our modern distinction between separation and divorce. In Graeco-Roman culture divorce could take place with or without legal documents. It could be brought about by the equivalent of the Jewish certificate of divorce, but it could be just as effectively established by simply leaving one's partner. Marriage and living with one another belonged together.

This is certainly the case in God's eyes. When Jesus was asked a question about divorce, he used the Greek word for 'separate' as the high point of his reply: 'What God has joined together, let man not separate' (Mark 10:9; Matthew 19:6). God has joined the couple together, they are to remain together.

Of course from a psychological point of view one is more final than the other. Reconciliation is much harder after there has been a divorce than when the couple are (only) separated. But reconciliation is also considerably harder after separation than when the couple are living together, however painfully. It is not true that, though he forbids divorce, God allows separation.

Can it be helpful to separate for a time?

Nevertheless, those seeking to help a friend in marriage difficulties often suggest a temporary separation. They say it may be helpful to have 'a cooling-off period' or 'to give each other space'.

It is an attractive idea. For many whose marriages seem like hell, any relief – even for a short time – seems worth clutching at. Perhaps one will gain emotional strength and so be better able to face the pressures and pain of the marriage.

In practice, separations are rarely helpful. They normally weaken the marriage. They give the clear message to the partner who is left that his wife/her husband is losing commitment to this relationship, and they often offer an immediate relief from suffering which is exhilarating and which continues to beckon strongly when the time of separation is over.

Still worse is a *trial* separation, 'to see if we would be better apart'. This is even more undermining of the marriage since it says explicitly that one partner at least is considering leaving permanently. It is often the catalyst that leads to the final breakdown of the marriage. Confidence has already been lost that the marriage can continue; the trial separation itself erodes any remaining confidence, and the marriage crumbles.

This is not to say that a brief separation is always a mistake. But for the Christian it must always be for a strictly limited, brief and, if at all possible, mutually agreed period with the express aim, clearly stated and understood right from the outset, that it is with a view to returning with fresh and renewed determination to make the marriage work. Compston suggests writing this aim down before the separation, and signing it.[5] Without this clear aim, a period of separation is far more likely to undermine, than to strengthen, the marriage.

What happens if I disobey Christ's teaching?

I am a Christian. I know that I have no moral grounds for divorcing my wife. She has not committed adultery; or if she has, I know that this would not be the real reason for leaving her, because if the relationship as a whole were happier, I could probably forgive her that. But I simply can't stand this marriage any longer. I feel I'm a shadow of the person I once was and could still be. I want desperately to leave her, even though I know that by Christ's standards it is wrong. So what happens if I leave her anyway? How will God regard me then?

The answer must be: with great sadness. God is a person, and it is possible to grieve him deeply (see Genesis 6:6; Psalm 78:40; Isaiah 63:10; Ephesians 4:30). He must grieve that we are wilfully disobeying him; he also grieves for the pain that we inflict on our partner (even though we may persuade ourselves that 'it will be better for him/her in the long run') and he grieves for all the other family members and friends that are deeply affected.

Yet doubtless God understands. He knows what it is to suffer intensely, to feel rejected, betrayed and deserted by those whom he'd given himself to most fully. Any marriage breakup certainly brings deep sadness to a wide circle of people, but God knows our feelings of being trapped and of screaming to get out; and where there is genuine repentance, of course he forgives. That repentance will normally mean seeking as full a reconciliation as possible with our partner, but it will not always be feasible to restore the marriage. Certainly, if we repent, God's forgiveness is total.

In any case, it is not for outsiders to judge. The story of the woman taken in adultery shows that clearly (John 8:3-11). Jesus does not exonerate the woman by saying that she has done nothing wrong. On the contrary, he tells her plainly that what she has done is sin and that she must abandon that way of life (v. 11). But he does forgive her – 'Neither do I condemn you' (v. 11) – and he makes it abundantly clear that this is between him and the woman; it is not for others to pass judgement (vv. 7-11).

This promise of Christ's mercy and forgiveness is a great comfort to those who have divorced their partners, though they now see (and perhaps saw then) that they were disobeying Christ. But it cannot be a reason for deliberately disobeying Christ now. We cannot knowingly sin because we are relying on Christ to forgive us when we have done so. Paul is horrified by the thought: 'What then? Shall we sin because we are not under law but under grace? By no means!' (Romans 6:15). And in any case, forgiveness in such a situation cannot be certain. God forgives not those who sin and hope to get away with it, but those who repent (e.g. Mark 1:4; Luke 24:46,47; Acts 3:19; 5:31).

How can I keep going in a loveless marriage?

It is hard. And in our bleakest moments we see years stretching before us, filled with bitterness, anger and pain.

But Christians have two great assets to keep them going and gradually to transform the situation. First, we have God himself. We have his friendship, his understanding, his listening to our frustration and our pain; we have his companionship in our suffering, because he has suffered deeply too.

But more than that, we have his help. He is not only willing us to make this marriage work, but he has promised us to honour what we attempt, and go on attempting, for him. It may mean humbling myself, it may mean asking my partner for forgiveness (even if I feel I have contributed less than half of the sin), it may mean being prepared to change more than I expect my partner to change. But God's promise stands: 'Those who honour me, I will honour' (1 Samuel 2:30).

Our second asset is other Christians. We need them, and they are a major part of God's provision for our support. This means that I, for my part, must be open with those closest to me as Christians; not with all, but with some. I must not put a brave face on it and pretend to everyone that all is well. I must not gradually withdraw from other people and hope I will be left alone. God has given me a Christian family precisely to keep me going in times like these, but I must be willing to open up and share my pain and my feelings of anger or guilt.

We who are the Christian family and friends of the sufferer need to be willing to listen; not to talk too much, not to advise, but to listen. Proverbs warns: 'He who answers before listening – that is his folly and shame' (Proverbs 18:13), and James adds: 'Everyone should be quick to listen, slow to speak and slow to become angry, for man's anger does not bring about the righteous life that God desires' (James 1:19,20). In this context of marital unhappiness, it is just as important for Christian friends not to get angry with the partner who is not present, or with whom we feel more of the fault lies, as it is to listen for a long, long time before we offer any advice to the partner we are with.

When we do eventually speak, let us be very wary of rebuke, because they are probably feeling guilty enough already. Let us be sure we have listened fully and carefully before we say anything about the way ahead. Let our words be few and full of encouragement; and let us offer to pray, both now – briefly – in their presence and every day in the weeks ahead.

With these assets – of good and unjudgemental Christian friends and of God himself – we do have the resources to obey Christ's often hard teaching, and keep going in a marriage where we regularly meet more indifference or anger than love.

The situation will, with God's help, almost imperceptibly change. Pressures do ease, the tension in the home isn't so constant, the really painful times are rarer and the better days become more frequent. Many old couples speak of the very rough time they had in their early or middle married years, from which they pulled through. Many divorced people, especially Christians, look back on their marriage and believe now that they could have made it work, with the help of Christ and the Christian family.

Many Christian couples are grateful that they did keep going through the most painful times. I've known for a long time a couple now in their forties. I've known them both since long before they were married. For several years their marriage was in very severe trouble; family members and many friends thought it would end in divorce, and that was certainly an idea that often crossed their minds, and sometimes their lips. But they knew the teaching of Christ and were determined to obey him. They prayed a great deal and sought help from Christians they respected, who gave them a better understanding of what was going on in their relationship. It was an uphill struggle and often their talking about their marriage simply led to further rows. But gradually they pulled through and today are happily, if not perfectly, married. Without Christ, they would almost certainly be divorced today. Through Christ, their troubled marriage has been healed.

Key verses

'"I hate divorce", says the Lord God of Israel' (Malachi 2:16).
'They are no longer two but one. Therefore what God has joined together, let man not separate' (Mark 10:8,9; Matthew 19:6).

CHAPTER 5

QUESTIONS ABOUT CHILDREN AND SEPARATION/DIVORCE

Brian and Emily's marriage was an empty shell. They managed to keep up appearances in public, and very few at their church would have guessed how desperate they felt, but in reality any spark of love had died long ago. They shared the same bedroom but hadn't had sex for over two years. They could talk about decorating the dining room or when they would take a family holiday, but any real sharing of feelings, hopes and fears had long since disappeared. And much of their communication was in petty sniping and mutual accusations.

There was no question that if they just consulted their own desires they would separate. But there were the children: Andrew (thirteen), Jenny (eleven) and Christopher (seven). How would the children react if the marriage broke up? And how long would they take to get over it? These questions about the children went round and round in Brian and Emily's minds.

What is the effect on children of separation and divorce?

All research shows that the permanent separation of their parents is initially devastating for children, and that the negative effects last far longer than parents ever hope or imagine, stretching well into adulthood.

Typical reactions are bewilderment, because they don't understand what is happening to their family and any explanations seem quite inadequate; depression, because the future seems unutterably bleak; anger, at one or both parents; a sense of rejection, because the parent who has left seems no longer to want them; guilt, because they blame themselves for causing their parent to leave; fear, that they may lose one or both parents completely; insecurity, because all the certainties of life have suddenly been taken away; regression, into behaviour which they grew out of some months or years before; loneliness, because one parent has left completely and the other seems to have less time for the children; underachievement at school; and day-dreaming, often associated with fantasising about, or planning, how their parents can be reconciled.

This is a dispiriting list, and while almost every child of divorce will show several of these reactions (sometimes concealed by pretending that nothing serious has happened or by becoming hyperactive and taking charge of the home), obviously not all will be present in an acute form.

Yet parents will frequently deny that their children are suffering in any but the most minor of ways. They see some symptoms but they downplay their importance.

We have to acknowledge that many parents have a vested interest in believing that the children are not seriously affected. The parent who took the initiative in the separation wants to assuage his (or her) sense of guilt and needs to assure himself that the children are not suffering much, that they will get over any initial pain and that the separation is in their best interests. The custodial parent wants to feel that she* is doing a good job and shielding the children from any harmful effects of the

---

* To save constant clumsiness in the writing, this chapter throughout assumes what is true in the majority of cases: that the mother is the custodial parent and the father is the visiting parent. Most of this chapter remains valid if the roles are reversed.

separation. And her friends also want to encourage her by saying that 'the children are coping remarkably well'.

Yet those who are able to be more objective – doctors, teachers and family friends – often know that the children are suffering deeply, though they will not acknowledge it to either parent. The Bible recognises that the greatest purely human pain is when 'my father and mother forsake me' (Psalm 27:10), and that is what most children feel has happened.

There is much truth in what they are feeling. Christopher Compston writes: 'If the children's interests were truly considered, the parents wouldn't divorce at all. By continuing their [plans to divorce], they have firmly put their interests before those of the children.'[6]

Isn't it better for children to live with one parent in peace, rather than with two who are constantly rowing?

Of course it is better for a child to be brought up in a peaceful environment. No one would dispute that a child brought up in a calm home with happily married parents has a better chance of developing healthily than the child of a home where the parents are constantly arguing. Wouldn't it therefore be better for the children if parents at loggerheads with each other split up and left the children to live with one parent in an atmosphere of real peace?

In the large majority of cases, the answer is no. For a start, the home of a newly divorced person is often not a place of peace. As we shall see in the next chapter, separation and divorce most frequently lead to turmoil and depression even in the partner who initiated the separation, and this frequently leads to a less healthy relationship between parent and child. Wallerstein and Kelly, in their meticulous study of the effects of divorce on families, found that although most parents had achieved some psychological stability five years after the divorce, in 40% of cases the mother's relationship with the children had deteriorated or remained poor throughout this period.[7]

But it is also true that the pre-divorce family, despite the parents' anger and fighting, is often a less traumatic place for the children than the parents imagine. Children are normally able to isolate themselves to a considerable extent (not completely) from their parents' arguments. That is one reason why the parents' separation is in most cases an enormous shock to the children, even if they have witnessed many scenes of intense anger, shouting and violence.

For almost all children the separation of their parents brings a marked set-back in their normal, healthy development. Some gradually recover from this set-back, others do not. It is true, of course, that after a period of years some children are making good progress and a minority are developing even more strongly than in the pre-divorce family.

Nevertheless, if you consulted the children themselves, especially at any stage in the first five years and very frequently thereafter, almost all would say that they would have preferred their parents to stay together. Wallerstein and Kelly can say: 'Only a few of the children in our study thought their parents were happily married, yet the overwhelming majority preferred the unhappy marriage to the divorce.'[8]

This fact is seen in another form: the children frequently cherish hopes of their parents' reconciliation long after the divorce and often even after one parent has remarried. Martin Richards has carried out one of the most extensive UK studies of the effect of divorce on children. He says: 'Separating parents often do not talk to their children and ask them what they want.' His interviewer asks him what children do want. Richards replies: 'They almost always say they only want one thing: that their parents should stay together' (*The Times*, 2 May 1995).

Isn't time a great healer?

Yes, time does heal. The acute phase of intense inner turmoil and bewilderment does pass. Children and adults gradually function better. But, perhaps surprisingly, the adults involved – the separating partners themselves – normally make a better and swifter recovery than the children.

In Wallerstein and Kelly's study, the family members and others involved with them (for example, the children's teachers) were interviewed soon after separation, eighteen months later and five years later. In a number of ways, the children were actually doing worse at five years than after eighteen months. For example, a higher percentage were 'consciously and intensely unhappy and dissatisfied with their life in the post-divorce family' (over one third of the children), and a higher percentage had feelings of 'intense loneliness' (27%). This was particularly true of adolescent boys, who tended to grow more angry about their parents' divorce as they moved into adolescence.[9]

Of course some children slowly recover and begin to develop well. Wallerstein and Kelly found that at five years after divorce about one third of the children were well adjusted while one third were still very unhappy, lonely and angry. But they also found that almost all the children, including those doing very well, 'had the sense of having sustained a difficult and unhappy time in their lives which had cast a shadow over their childhood and adolescence . . . For all, a significant part of their childhood or their adolescence had been a sad and frightening time.'[10]

The effects of divorce on children go on and on. Jack Dominian quotes several different studies which have shown that there is a very considerably higher rate of suicide, criminality and marital breakdown in the adult children of divorce than in the general adult population.[11]

**Do some children fully support their parents' divorce
and wish it had happened sooner?**

It is rare for children to be in favour of their parents' divorce,
especially if the children are still living at home. The vast
majority wish that their parents would stay together or get back
together and perceive their intact family – despite the physical
violence they may well have witnessed – as the place where they
have received the support and protection they need.

In a number of cases, with greater distance in time and more
independence from their parents, children come to see their
parents' divorce as inevitable and beneficial. They may see, for
example, that it has brought greater happiness to one or both
parents.

But these same children may be unaware of the continuing
effect of the divorce on themselves. Martin Richards and his
Cambridge team have been following the development of
17,000 children born in Britain in one week in 1958. He has
found, for example, that middle-class children of divorce are
twice as likely to leave school without any qualifications and
considerably more likely to have no full-time job at the age of
twenty-three. Children of divorce are also twice as likely to be
married or living with someone before the age of twenty and
twice as likely to have a child before the same age. And children
of divorce are much more likely to divorce themselves.

In the light of these facts we have to conclude that, while a
number of children come eventually to approve their parents'
divorce, it has not been for the short- or long-term benefit of the
large majority of children themselves.

**Is the welfare of the children a good enough reason
for staying together?**

But children aren't the only pebbles on the beach. The parents
have their own needs and longings, and they may feel strongly

that the only way out of their intolerable pain would be to separate. So as a desperate wife or husband thinks about the future, are the interests of the children a sufficient reason for staying together?

Yes, they are. Jesus said, 'If any of you put a stumbling block before one of these little ones who believe in me, it would be better for you if a great millstone were fastened around your neck and you were drowned in the depth of the sea' (Matthew 18:6, NRSV). Scholars are divided as to whether, when Jesus talks about 'these little ones', he means 'children' or 'his disciples who are to be like humble children'. But it really makes little difference. Either Jesus is in fact talking about children or he is talking about people who are to be like children; and in either case he is saying that to 'put a stumbling block' before a child (or someone who is childlike) is so appalling that it would be better to drown yourself than to do it.

Parents are called by God to protect their children from harm. It must be right, therefore, for parents to stay together 'for the sake of the children', even if it means continuing pain for themselves.

But this of course is not the only reason for staying together. A still higher reason is because this is God's plainly stated will. Jesus said, 'What God has joined together, let man not separate' (Mark 10:9; Matthew 19:6). A Christian husband or wife will determine to stay within an awful marriage not only for the sake of the children but for the sake of God their heavenly Father.

Some couples, because of their children, make up their minds that they will just hang on until the children have grown up and left home. They have become resigned to the idea that the marriage will never work, they will cease to put any effort into trying to make things better; it is for them an enormous sacrifice just to keep going for several more years. This is very understandable and may be all a couple can contemplate at the moment. But it underestimates the effect of their parents' divorce on children who have left home. At any age, it is normally devastating, a betrayal of all the family stood for.

Simply hanging on in a marriage cannot be enough for the Christian. At the end of one of the most famous New Testament passages on marriage, Paul sums up: 'Each one of you also must love his wife as he loves himself, and the wife must respect her husband' (Ephesians 5:33).

This can be enormously difficult when almost all love and respect have drained out of the marriage. Nevertheless, it must be every Christian's desire, prayer and attempt to build new love and to discover new respect. And it does happen. Christians who for several years have only been able to hang on in a marriage have often seen their relationship slowly begin to revive, with the help and encouragement of others.

How may I feel about letting the children see their dad or live with their mum?

These next questions assume that you are already separated, or perhaps divorced. If you are the mum, you may feel desperate about your children seeing their dad. You may disapprove of his morals and lifestyle, the children may return from visits clearly upset and difficult to handle, you may have a strong and perhaps accurate suspicion that he is telling your children vicious and untrue stories about you. If it were any other man, you would certainly ensure that all contact between him and your children were cut off, so why should it be any different because he happens to be their father?

If you are the dad, you may feel equally desperate that your children are living with their mother rather than you. If you initiated the separation, you wanted, all things considered, to be free of your wife but you didn't want to lose the children. If your wife left you, it seems so totally unjust that she should not only break up the marriage but keep the children. And again you may fear, perhaps rightly, that your wife is poisoning their minds against you.

These factors help to explain why half of all fathers lose contact with their children within two to three years from the separation. But the facts are somewhat different from what the parents imagine. Over the question of morals and lifestyle, for example, Wallerstein and Kelly discovered: 'The conflict in values between the parents, which often stirred them to great anger, did not pose insolvable problems for the children we observed. Often the children were relatively unaware of, and certainly unconcerned about, some of the differences that most angered the adults, such as differences in sexual mores, in modesty, in nudity or in manners.'[12]

The most important fact is that for children to develop healthily they need a loving, open relationship with both their mother and their father, seeing both as regularly as possible. No other adult, however caring, is a substitute for the dad (or mum). It therefore does much more harm to children to restrict their father's access to them than to allow them regularly to see an individual whom you regard as disruptive or even poisonous.

Christopher Compston sums this up well. Access is not primarily the visiting parent's right; he may in fact find it very painful to visit and want to diminish, or put an end to, his visits. But access is the child's right.[13]

What if the children have to move home or schools?

Following a divorce the children often have to move home and change schools. This doesn't necessarily happen immediately but it is common in the first eighteen months after separation, either because the marital home has to be sold and the proceeds divided or because the mum moves in with a new boyfriend or husband.

It is certainly disruptive to the children. Their world has suddenly fallen apart in a way that they neither desired nor (whatever they may think) were responsible for. Their house, with its familiar rooms, is at least one point of continuity. And so is the school; its routine and discipline may be invaluable at a time when family life has become so unpredictable and family routine may be non-existent.

But study after study shows emphatically that home and school are not the most important factors in a child's welfare and psychological health. Rather, it is his or her continuing relationship with both father and mother.

If children are not able to see both parents regularly, or if the parents' anger with one another means that time with their father is overshadowed by the bitter exchanges or the heavy silences when they are picked up or when they are dropped off again, then they are likely to cope very badly with the divorce and find their normal development arrested. But if the parents, at whatever pain to themselves, are able to allow each other (virtually) unrestricted access to the children, and if the parents can manage to remain civil with each other, especially in the children's presence, then the damage to the children will be much less, and largely normal psychological growth may be able to resume after a time.

What effect would my marrying again have on the children?

Children normally find the remarriage of either parent intensely disturbing. If their father remarries, the effect is almost always to distance him from them. He wants, and needs, to devote much of his time outside work to his new wife. If she has children, he wants to establish a relationship with them, especially if – as is normally the case – he and they are now living together. The result is that he has less time for the children of his first marriage.

This weakening of ties with their father may be secretly desired, or actively encouraged, by the mother who may see it as a way of finally getting him out of their life or who resents another woman having a strong influence over her children. But the children experience it as a second rejection by their father, painful and detrimental to their psychological health, even if – or rather, especially if – they roundly declare that they want nothing more to do with him.

If, by contrast, the father seeks to maintain regular and undiminished contact with his children, it frequently puts very great strains on his new marriage.

If the mother remarries, the children's normal reaction is to resent the intruder. There is often the feeling that 'I have lost my dad, now I'm losing my mum too', especially if the new couple spend a lot of time alone together and the children feel excluded. This sense of betrayal and loss can be equally present if the mum has a live-in boyfriend.

Of course there are exceptions, especially with the passage of time. Some children become very attached to their stepfather, rather fewer to their stepmother. But a stepfather is no substitute for dad, and it remains essential that the children have regular, unhindered access to their own father.

The father frequently finds this more difficult with another man living under the same roof as his children and married to their mother. It is not surprising therefore that many parents, who would remarry if they consulted only their own wishes, decide to forego a new relationship so as to put nothing in the way of the children's continuing closeness to both their mother and their father.

How can I most support my children?

If you are already divorced, there are three ways in particular in which you can support your children and encourage them to cope as well as possible with the situation they find themselves in. First, you can ensure that the non-custodial parent (whether this is you or your ex-partner) has as easy, regular, open and flexible access to the children as possible. If you are the non-custodial dad, this means arranging your timetable around your visits with the children: making sure you are there at the time agreed, never cancelling if at all possible, seeing them as often as their mum will allow. It may even mean leaving a job, and certainly not accepting a new job, which will take you away from where they live.

If you are the custodial mum, it means allowing access to their dad as frequently as possible, not insisting on rigidly sticking to the letter of the law, letting their dad come into your home at bathtime and bedtime, if you can bear it.

The Bible sees it as one of the great tragedies of life to be fatherless. God cares deeply for those who are without fathers. He is 'a father to the fatherless'; he 'defends' and 'helps' them (Psalm 68:5; 10:14,18; compare 146:9). He expects us to defend them too: 'Take your evil deeds out of my sight! Stop doing wrong, learn to do right! . . . Defend the cause of the fatherless' (Isaiah 1:16,17). Of course these passages are thinking principally of children whose fathers have died; but being robbed of a father by divorce is often even more devastating than losing him through death.

Secondly, you can support your children by having as good a relationship as possible with your divorced partner. You destroy your children's respect for you, you ruin any pleasure they may have in their other parent's company and you slow down their emotional healing if you continue to have bitter exchanges with one another. By contrast, your children are much more likely gradually to resume normal, healthy development if their parents are civil and accommodating with each other.

Thirdly, you support your children if you rigidly forbid yourself to speak badly of your divorced partner not only to, but in the presence of, your children – even if you are well aware that he is speaking badly of you in their presence. It can be enormously difficult continually to bite your tongue, but it is very much in the interests of your children and their happiness that you do so.

Best of all, if you want to support your children, is to stay together; or, if you are already separated or divorced, to talk about and explore any mutually agreed ways of trying to get back together. In nine cases out of ten, this is what your children long for. And if, with God's help and over a period of time, you can make it work, it will undoubtedly be best for your children.

Key verses

'Do not grieve the Holy Spirit of God, with whom you were sealed for the day of redemption. Get rid of all bitterness, rage and anger, brawling and slander, along with every form of malice. Be kind and compassionate to one another, forgiving each other, just as in Christ God forgave you' (Ephesians 4:30-32).

CHAPTER 6

QUESTIONS ABOUT THE EFFECT ON ME OF SEPARATION/DIVORCE

Colin had taken a long time deciding to leave his wife. He had first thought about it only a short time after their marriage and it had been on his mind almost continually over the last six months. Finally, he spoke to her one evening and left the following weekend.

This was not an impulsive decision; he believed he had thought through every aspect of it, and he was generous in providing for Jenny and willing to fit around her convenience for when he could see the children. But although he was thankfully free of the constant friction in the home, he was also desperately lonely and missing the children far more than he had imagined. It seemed he had gone into a long, dark cave and got lost. He thought he'd taken charge of his life and was disconcertingly completely adrift. How long would this nightmare go on?

What are the emotional benefits of separation/divorce?

Colin had anticipated benefits from the separation. In fact, he thought it would be better for all the family in the long run. Was he wrong? Surely there are benefits in separating, so that some people look back on their divorce as a wise, though painful, decision?

There are benefits, and Colin himself was experiencing some of those which come immediately. Relief may well be the initial reaction, especially in the partner who has taken the initiative in separating. At last the months of agonising indecision are over; at last there has been some decisive action. One or both partners may feel a measure of peace, mixed in with their inner turmoil; at least there aren't the constant raised voices or accusing silences. And some partners feel a heady sense of new-found freedom; this is more often felt by men and is rarely experienced immediately by a custodial parent with children.

But many of these initial benefits of separation are felt much more strongly by one partner than by the other, who may well see the separation as an almost unmitigated disaster. And many of the positive reactions either do not last or are submerged, as Colin was finding, by much greater problems.

The picture may be different some years later. While divorce is always painful for both partners, for the children, for family and for friends, there are benefits in the long term for some divorcees. Some, for example, develop a new self-esteem. This is quite often the case with those women who re-enter part or full-time employment, hesitantly at first, and find that they thrive in a demanding job while at the same time bringing up a family and looking after the home.

Some men find that they become better parents, developing a closer relationship with their children than they had while the family was intact. Many more men, of course, find their relationship with their children strained, or lose contact with them altogether. But some derive new-found pleasure in being dads and thereby gain in self-confidence.

Above all, some divorcees find that their pain and helplessness propel them to seek for, and find, God. Some discover him for the first time. Others are led much deeper in their experience of him. Tom Jones writes that at first his 'aloneness' was 'raw pain', then 'a comfortable place to hide', and finally 'a new opportunity to discover myself . . . My aloneness became my teacher . . . I came to experience a much deeper and more personal relationship with God than I had ever known before'.[14]

This is precisely what God has promised: 'The Lord is close to the broken-hearted and saves those who are crushed in spirit' (Psalm 34:18). His love is especially offered to those who suffer deeply, and our churches contain many who have found Christ in their pain.

So for a whole variety of reasons – negatively because they are free of the strains of an intolerable marriage, and positively because of the constructive changes in their own character, independence or faith – several divorcees look back on the separation as beneficial, overall, for their lives.

What are the emotional wounds of separation/divorce?

But the wounds are many and various. Although some people come to see the benefits as outweighing the pain, many would never have separated if they had known the emotional hell they would have to go through.

One of the wounds of separation is a deep sense of failure. Jones describes this well from his own experience:

> Suddenly, I was feeling like a failure in almost every aspect of my life. I failed at marriage, and soon I began to feel like a failure as a father . . . I felt that I no longer had what it took to fulfil my calling [as an ordained minister] . . . Therefore, I left the ministry and felt like a failure before God. Of course I was out of work and began to feel like a financial failure. In time, I made some foolish decisions in relationships with women, and I felt like a moral failure. That only added to my sense of being a total failure before God.[15]

Confidence in yourself sinks to rock bottom. 'Rejection by the one you love . . . is the most powerful destroyer of self-esteem in the entire realm of human experience.'[16]

Another wound is intense loneliness, often far more deeply felt than the separating partners anticipated. One woman wrote to me that what hit her hardest was being so alone, especially coming in from work and at bedtime: 'Not having anyone to share with: thoughts, ideas, daily happenings; not having anyone to share decisions – especially over the children; not having anyone to do practical things: mend/repair, give lifts, meet the children; not having anyone to cuddle, show affection to, be interested in.'

People react to this loneliness in a variety of different ways: some submerge themselves in work, returning home as late as possible; some launch into a hectic social and sexual life; some retreat from all human relationships; some begin to drink too much; some move in with a new partner or remarry long before they are emotionally ready for any such relationship.

Depression is a further wound of marital separation. A man said to me:

> I couldn't concentrate on anything for very long and was ultrasensitive to criticism . . . Because of my increasing depression, I became isolated and withdrawn. I found it difficult to be part of all the normal activities that I had previously enjoyed. I even found music to be of little help, to the point where sitting and listening to music actually increased my sadness . . . None of these after-effects were things I had ever considered when thinking about a breakup . . . I had foolishly imagined that life would be much the same as before, with the difference that Karen wouldn't be there and thus harmony would be restored.

Feelings of guilt can be overpowering. One woman told me: 'I blamed myself for everything; any accident was my fault; the rebelliousness of my teenage daughters was all because of our divorce.' This led to a breakdown 'which took me two years to climb out of. Those two years were what I imagine hell to be'.

The sense of being guilty is just as likely to strike the partner who has had no hand in the separation. One woman to her utter amazement discovered on her birthday that her husband had left her. At first she was 'completely shell-shocked . . . About ten months later I began to feel guilty and that I must be a wicked person . . . I didn't go to church because I felt evil and unclean'.

At the same time there is often fierce anger and bitterness. One woman relates how, before planned meetings with her husband, 'I would tremble and feel sick', and if she met him unexpectedly, 'I normally experienced extreme emotions: fear, embarrassment, hostility . . . I would feel that my new [remarried] life had been invaded and I was angry.' Even now, many years on, the mere sight of her first husband can make her tremble with rage.

Christians react to the wounds of separation in different ways. Some, as we have seen, find God drawing close to them. Others, especially if they have taken the initiative in separating, withdraw from the Church and abandon any clear faith in God. They often feel guilty before God, even if they will not acknowledge it; they also feel that God has let them down.

This is especially tragic, because God is pre-eminently someone who understands suffering at first hand: 'He was despised and rejected by men, a man of sorrows, and familiar with suffering. Like one from whom men hide their faces he was despised, and we esteemed him not' (Isaiah 53:3). He is the compassionate and understanding friend of all who themselves feel worthless and abandoned.

How long does it take to get over the wounds?

Healing does take place. The acute pain of the first eighteen months doesn't go on for ever. It's important to realise this, because like Colin (quoted at the beginning of this chapter), you can feel you have entered a deep, dark cavern and there is no way out. Many have thoughts of suicide in these early months.

The healing normally takes much longer than we hope or imagine, and there are often major relapses. In fact, it is dangerous to feel too early that you are beginning to cope. You may well find that fresh problems suddenly devastate you. A woman wrote: 'I felt really happy [after our separation] for the first time for years. Three months later, suddenly and without warning, I began to suffer severe depression and felt weighed down by the responsibilities which now piled on me.'

It is often reckoned that the worst period is the first two to three years, with the men often recovering rather more quickly than the women. Wallerstein and Kelly found in their study that eighteen months after the separation, men were likely to be more positive about the marriage breakup than they had been initially; the women, by contrast, were divided about how they saw the separation, and a higher percentage of them were negative about it than at the time when the separation took place.[17] This may be because more of the women took the final decision to separate; they were disillusioned as they discovered that the reality didn't match up to their initial hopes.

By contrast, five years on from the separation Wallerstein and Kelly found that some of the women were doing better than the men. Although, still, '31% of the men and 42% of the women had not yet achieved psychological or social stability', 'fewer men [than women] seemed to have utilised the divorce experience to bring about positive change in their lives'. Women had worked harder at making positive changes to their lives and about 25% of them had 'undergone striking and significant positive changes that appeared to have lifelong implications'.[18]

However, you are never completely healed of the wounds of divorce, not in this life. I have just heard today of a young man killed in a car crash. His father, a man I respect enormously for his Christian maturity, divorced the young man's mother over twenty-five years ago. But this death has brought all the guilt, the sense of failure as husband and father and some of the bitterness flooding back. Divorce scars you for life and the wounds are easily reopened at any time.

But over the months and years there will be healing. It is very important that you give yourself, and give God, time. As after a major operation, most of us want to be back and fully coping far too early. It only leads to further hurt and disappointment. The Psalmist was wiser: 'I waited patiently for the Lord; he turned to me and heard my cry. He lifted me out of the slimy pit, out of the mud and mire; he set my feet on a rock and gave me a firm place to stand. He put a new song in my mouth, a hymn of praise to our God. Many will see and fear and put their trust in the Lord' (Psalm 40:1-3). The first words are the most important: 'I waited patiently for the Lord.'

What effect is the legal system likely to have on us?

Sadly, the involvement of lawyers often increases the bitterness of divorce. Good legal advice may be necessary, of course, but leaving negotiations to both partners' lawyers normally makes the marriage breakup more painful for everyone involved.

Quite frequently, one partner – normally the wife – goes to a solicitor in order to give her husband a shock; it is a cry to be heard and to take their marriage problems seriously. But very often the legal process, once begun, develops a momentum of its own; Compston, himself a judge, likens it to a snowball running downhill. The husband receives a curt solicitor's letter; he reacts angrily and, without either party really wanting it, they are into divorce proceedings.

It is a cardinal principle for all marriage counsellors to remain neutral. It is equally a cardinal principle for lawyers to be partisan. They are trained to fight for their client and to take comparatively little account of the other party's feelings or needs. In such an adversarial atmosphere, bitterness inevitably escalates.

The court settlement often doesn't end matters. There are frequently further tussles over money and access to the children. In America, especially, these often end up back in court. That is why current UK Government legislation seeks to promote the use of Family Mediation. The hope is that more couples will sit down with professional mediators whose aim will be to help them reach fair and mutually agreed arrangements, with as little acrimony as possible. Before the new legislation it was reckoned that between six and ten per cent of couples used a mediation (or conciliation) service. It is hoped that now this may rise to forty per cent.

It is, therefore, best to avoid reaching decisions through lawyers if at all possible. Jesus himself spoke about human anger and said: 'Settle matters quickly with your adversary who is taking you to court. Do it while you are still with him on the way, or he may hand you over to the judge . . . and you may be thrown into prison. I tell you the truth, you will not get out until you have paid the last penny' (Matthew 5:25,26).

Divorce proceedings are not likely to land you in prison; but they may well cost you considerable sums in lawyer's fees and will very likely cause great bitterness to you, your partner and your children.

How will I be affected financially?

Many men, and nearly all women, are substantially poorer as a result of their divorce. It is the women whose finances are hit particularly hard. Especially if they have children, their earning power is often substantially less than their former partner's, and what he provides for the children frequently seems to bear little relation to what they cost. In any case, many men simply give up paying after a time. Studies show that in the USA fewer than half the men are still paying anything for their children one year after the divorce. And in Britain, the Child Support Agency has been set up because so many non-custodial parents are defaulting on payments for their children.

Wendy Green has this advice for those who are thinking about separation: 'Look around your home. How would you feel if it had to be split with someone else? . . . Could you manage on half your present income?'[19]

Sadly, money is often the cause of greatly increased bitterness. The partner who has been left may feel that it is the ultimate insult that the partner who leaves can take half the money and possessions. The leaving partner is often at first most generous over financial arrangements, out of a sense of guilt at breaking up the marriage. But once his (or her) feeling of guilt has worn off, he is likely to feel bitter about having 'given everything away', and he may well want to renegotiate.

How will friends react to me?

The reaction of your friends will vary enormously. Some will prove real bricks. Their acceptance and continuing love will be a vital part of your healing process. This undiminished, or even increased, commitment is, of course, what true friendship is all about: 'A friend loves at all times, and a brother is born for adversity' (Proverbs 17:17).

Though you will probably particularly rely on one or two close friends, you will need to keep in touch with as many friends as possible, even though your natural inclination may be to retreat into your shell. One woman told me: 'Friends listened and phoned. I began to use different friends for different purposes: cheering up, calming down, practical support, spiritual wrestling and general chewing the cud. Some friends took the four of us [she has three children] camping in Normandy with them – that was a wonderful break.'

But other former friends will prove a grave disappointment. The Psalms know all about this: 'My friends and companions avoid me because of my wounds; my neighbours stay far away' (Psalm 38:11). Some will avoid you because they do not know what to say; you may see them crossing the road so as not to meet you ('I am a dread to my friends – those who see me on the street flee from me' [Psalm 31:11]). Some will drop you from their normal invitations because, as a single person, you don't fit in with their seating plan or perhaps because a friend's wife sees you as a threat since you are now (she believes) sexually available. Others, again, will take your partner's side and be fiercely critical of you: 'Even my close friend, whom I trusted, he who shared my bread, has lifted up his heel against me' (Psalm 41:9).

When a divorce takes place, not only the furniture and money but the friends too get divided up between the partners. Very few friends will stay in touch with you both.

But if you are a Christian, you should have faithful friends who will stick by you, and one or two in particular who will be willing to spend a great deal of time with you, listening, supporting and listening again. Proverbs 18:24 is often applied to Christ, but it was written originally to commend all faithful, godly friends: 'Some friends play at friendship but a true friend sticks closer than one's nearest kin' (NRSV).

How will my partner's family react to me?

It is not easy to predict how your partner's parents, and the rest of his family, will react to you. You may find that they take their child's (or sibling's) side and paint you as the villain, especially if it was you who finally decided to make the break. This is how Samson's father-in-law reacted initially to him (Judges 14:15–15:2), even though later, out of fear of Samson, he tried to placate his son-in-law.

You may equally find, especially if you are the one who has been left, that one or more of your partner's family is very kind and that they refuse to take sides. If you have children, try for their sake to keep in touch with your partner's parents, even if you feel that you yourself cannot bear to meet them. Your children need as close a relationship as possible with both sets of grandparents.

How will God react to me?

Whether Christian or not, most divorcees feel guilty about what they have done. For Christians, it is often worse. They feel they have let God down, broken the solemn vows they took before him and brought disgrace on the name of Christ. They have ringing in their ears God's stark words: 'I hate divorce' (Malachi 2:16). So how does God react to me if my partner and I are separated?

That must depend on your own attitude. If you are defiant, not prepared to acknowledge that you contributed anything to the breakdown of the marriage, or knowing that there were no biblical grounds for the separation but refusing even to think about reconciliation, then there is not much that God can do to help you. Certainly he understands the pain that you are going through, but he is surely sad that you have cut yourself off from his will and his love. 'All day long I have held out my hands to a disobedient and obstinate people' (Romans 10:21).

But if (as is much more likely, if you are reading this book) you are humble and broken and looking to him for help, if you are only too aware of your faults in the marriage and are looking to be forgiven, you can be quite certain of his compassion, his complete forgiveness and his unhesitating acceptance.

As we saw in Chapter 1, it was said of Jesus: 'A bruised reed he will not break, and a smouldering wick he will not snuff out' (Matthew 12:20). This is the very opposite of the normal attitude in today's throw-away society, where anything substandard – whether material a craftsman might have used (a bruised reed) or part of a night light beginning to burn low (a smouldering wick) or a human being broken by divorce – is simply thrown on the scrap heap. Jesus, by contrast, cares for people who are bruised and nurses them back to healthy life (the context of Matthew 12:20 is quiet, unostentatious healing; see verses 15 and 16). He nurtures those whose spiritual life has almost petered out and gently restores its earlier, brighter flame.

Far from having finished with you, he is wanting to deepen your life with him (though this may take time; don't be impatient with yourself or him), and he will use you again in his service. It was a woman who had been divorced five times whom Christ used to spread his good news through a whole town in Samaria (John 4:17, 18, 28, 29, 39-41).

How can I use my experience to help other people?

You know at first hand what it is to be separated and divorced. You probably feel that several of your friends tried to be sympathetic and caring but didn't really understand. Now someone you know and love – a friend, a neighbour, a family member – is going through the pain of separation. Each story and situation is different, of course, but there is much that you do understand; you can genuinely enter into many of their feelings.

It's not surprising that those who most help the newly separated are those who have been through a separation themselves. Above all they can listen with understanding, they will probably have the wisdom not to say too much, and their few words and personal experience may prove a great encouragement. One woman's story is typical: another divorcee befriended her and 'she turned my inner despair and desperation to hope'.

This principle receives its highest expression in Jesus himself. 'Because he himself suffered when he was tempted, he is able to help those who are being tempted' (Hebrews 2:18). The fact that he has been through temptation makes him 'sympathetic', 'merciful' and 'helpful' (see these words in Hebrews 4:14-16) when we are going through our own temptations.

We are not Jesus, of course. We can and must never take his place and must always seek gently to point in his direction anyone who is suffering. But we are those who have suffered ourselves and know the temptations, struggles and bitterness that others who have more recently separated are going through. And therefore we are uniquely placed to offer support and help.

Hosier calls Jesus 'the wounded healer' and says that those who have been through separation and divorce are called by Christ to be wounded healers too. Loneliness is difficult and painful, but it can be used to understand myself and to reach out to others who are suffering. I can be a healer because I myself am wounded and therefore understand what it is to be in pain.[20]

In our own church family a group for the separated and divorced (Oasis) is run entirely by those who are themselves divorced. It has proved a lifeline to many divorcees, both from within the church and from the wider community. The leaders of the group are putting their own painful experience to use in serving others.*

This practice of using our own pain, and how Christ has met us in it, to help others is exactly what Paul talks about in 2 Corinthians 1:3-7 – 'Praise be to the God and Father of our Lord Jesus Christ, the Father of compassion and the God of all comfort, who comforts us in all our troubles, so that we can comfort those in any trouble with the comfort we ourselves have received from God . . . And our hope for you is firm, because we know that just as you share in our sufferings, so also you share in our comfort.'

You will never be happy about the pain you have been through, but you will be grateful to God that you can use it to strengthen others who are suffering; and they will be grateful to God for you.

Key verses

Jesus said, 'Come to me, all you who are weary and burdened, and I will give you rest. Take my yoke upon you and learn from me, for I am gentle and humble in heart, and you will find rest for your souls' (Matthew 11:28,29).

*Details of how Oasis is run can be obtained from Jim Wheeler, 7 Huntington Road, Crowborough, East Sussex TN6 2LJ.

CHAPTER 7

QUESTIONS ABOUT REMARRIAGE

Lewis was not a Christian when he married Fiona. They were married for ten years and increasingly grew apart. It was painful for Lewis but he had come to accept a home life that was not going to be particularly happy, so it came as a complete surprise to him when Fiona began talking in earnest about a divorce. Within a few months, she was gone.

Lewis found it infinitely more painful than he imagined. A colleague at work invited him to church and there he found love and acceptance, which was just what he needed. He also met Janet, a single woman in her late thirties and a very committed Christian. They fell in love and found that almost everyone was delighted with their burgeoning relationship, including most of the members of the church.

But they knew that Christ's teaching had traditionally been understood as forbidding remarriage while a divorcee's partner is still alive. They didn't want to go too far with their relationship before they knew whether God might allow them to get married. And they wanted to understand both the teaching of Christ and the reasons behind it.

Does God permit me to remarry?

Lewis and Janet were right: the New Testament teaching on remarriage comes almost entirely from the lips of Jesus. He taught on a number of occasions about remarriage after divorce. And when asked a question solely about divorce (Mark 10:2,10; Matthew 19:3), he deliberately also introduced the question of remarriage (Mark 10:11,12; Matthew 19:9-12).

His teaching is most clearly and succinctly summed up in Luke 16:18 – 'Anyone who divorces his wife and marries another woman commits adultery, and the man who marries a divorced woman commits adultery.' There is no doubt that this was Jesus' basic position: to remarry after divorce is, according to Jesus, breaking the seventh commandment ('You shall not commit adultery') and therefore forbidden by God; and for a single person to marry a divorcee is to break the same commandment of God.

The saying in Luke forbids a divorced man to remarry or a single man to marry a divorced woman. In Mark's Gospel a very similar saying of Christ's gives much the same teaching to both men and women: 'Anyone who divorces his wife and marries another woman commits adultery against her. And if she divorces her husband and marries another man, she commits adultery' (Mark 10:11,12).

Paul, who specifically says that he is quoting the teaching of Jesus, does not call remarriage 'adultery' but allows only two options to a divorcee: remaining single or being reconciled to one's partner. 'To the married I give this command (not I, but the Lord): A wife must not separate from her husband. But if she does, she must remain unmarried or else be reconciled to her husband. And a husband must not divorce his wife' (1 Corinthians 7:10,11).

The hard truth is that Jesus never spoke in favour of remarriage and, whenever he referred to it, he always called it 'adultery' (Matthew 5:32 [twice]; 19:9; Mark 10:11,12; Luke

16:18 [twice]). We have to conclude that Christ's fundamental answer to the question 'Does God permit a divorcee to remarry?' is 'no'.

But why? It seems so hard and uncompassionate. The common assumption is that Christ forbade remarriage because, for some reason, he believed that divorce is the unforgivable sin; or because he wanted to punish divorcees. This is emphatically not the case. It is vital to understand that Christ forbids remarriage after divorce not because of the nature of divorce but because of the nature of marriage.

This can clearly be seen in Christ's own teaching about divorce and remarriage. As we have already seen (in Chapter 3), when Christ was asked a question about divorce (Mark 10:2; Matthew 19:3), he refused to answer without first explaining God's understanding of marriage. In marriage, God joins the couple together and the couple become one flesh; the most important truth about them, in God's eyes, is that 'they are no longer two but one' (Mark 10:3-9; Matthew 19:4-8). This makes divorce no longer an option for the Christian (except that a Christian may divorce when there has been sexual infidelity: Matthew 5:32; 19:9), and it also has implications for remarriage.

Jesus consistently called remarriage after divorce 'adultery'. In Greek, as in English, there are two words for sex outside marriage. These are normally translated 'fornication' (i.e. sex when neither party is married) and 'adultery' (i.e. sex when at least one party is married).

Jesus deliberately uses this second word (*moicheia* in Greek) to describe remarriage after divorce. By doing so, he explains why remarriage is not permitted by God. Remarriage is not allowed because in God's eyes the first marriage has not been dissolved. It may no longer exist in the eyes of the secular law, but in God's eyes it does still exist. For this reason remarriage after divorce is *adultery,* because a divorcee is still from God's point of view married. Jesus shows very clearly that a divorced man is still married to his (legally divorced) wife when he says: 'Anyone who divorces his wife and marries another woman *commits adultery against her*' (Mark 10:11).

So the reason why Christ forbids remarriage is not because of the nature of divorce (not because it is some especially heinous sin) but because of the nature of marriage. A couple are joined together by God in marriage, they become one flesh, and only death – not divorce – can undo this work of God.

What if my partner committed adultery?

But is there no exception? We have seen (in Chapter 4) that Jesus' fundamental attitude on the question of divorce was that husbands and wives should not separate. But he did give one exception: he allowed divorce only on the grounds of marital unfaithfulness (Matthew 5:32; 19:9). Does this exception also apply to remarriage?

Everyone agrees that this can only be answered by a careful study of Matthew 19:9 in its context (Matthew 5:32 is too brief and provides too little evidence to come to any firm conclusion). If, then, we look at the whole incident in Matthew 19:1-12, we find that the discussion at first focuses exclusively on divorce. It is about divorce, not about remarriage, that the Pharisees ask (v. 3).

Jesus does not immediately reply to their question about divorce. Instead, he insists on teaching them about marriage. God created human beings with a view to marriage; in marriage they become no longer two but one; God joins the husband and wife together (vv. 4-6a). So the answer to their question about divorce is: 'What God has joined together, let man not separate' (v. 6b).

The Pharisees then object: surely Moses in the law gave a 'command' about divorce (v. 7)? Jesus replies that Moses did indeed 'permit' divorce but only because the Israelites were hard-hearted. This was certainly not God's original, or lasting, intention (v. 8).

To underline the point, Jesus says: 'I tell you that anyone who divorces his wife, except for marital unfaithfulness, and marries another woman commits adultery' (v. 9). The main thrust of his teaching is unmistakable. He is wanting to reiterate, in answer to their question (v. 3), that God's basic stance is: no divorce. He adds to this the new thought that to remarry after divorce is to disobey God in a further way: it is to commit adultery.

The exception ('except for marital unfaithfulness') is very much an aside. It is natural that we should focus on it: we want to know when divorce, and if remarriage, is allowed. But Jesus is principally answering their question about divorce and is principally giving God's 'no' to divorce.

Yet clearly there is an exception here. Is Jesus saying, 'God says no to divorce, except where there has been unfaithfulness, and no to remarriage under any circumstances'? Or is he saying, 'God says no to divorce, except where there has been unfaithfulness, and no to remarriage, except where there has been unfaithfulness'? Both are possible grammatically, in Greek and English.

Two facts above all convince me that the first interpretation is correct: Jesus is teaching: 'God says no to divorce, except where there has been unfaithfulness, and no to remarriage under any circumstances'.

The first is *the disciples' surprise*. Immediately after Jesus has given his teaching about divorce and remarriage, 'The disciples said to him, "If this is the situation between a husband and wife, it is better not to marry"' (v. 10). They are clearly taken aback by what he has said; they didn't expect it and find it objectionable.

But if Jesus is saying that divorce is only permitted where there has been unfaithfulness and that in that case remarriage is also permitted, they shouldn't have been surprised at all. In Jesus' day the question of divorce was hotly debated among the Jews. One school followed Rabbi Hillel in saying that a man could divorce his wife for any reason, however trivial. Another school, following Rabbi Shammai, said that a man could divorce his wife only for sexual immorality. Both schools of thought were well known and in fact Jesus was being asked by the Pharisees which side he came down on (v. 3). And both schools taught that where God permits divorce, he permits remarriage also.

Clearly Jesus was known to have strict views on divorce. The Pharisees only asked the question 'to test him' (v. 3) and were asking it specifically in the part of Palestine where the ruler was the Herod who married Herodias (v. 1). Both Herod and Herodias were divorced. John the Baptist had already been arrested and killed by them for opposing their marriage (Matthew 14:3,4) and the Pharisees doubtless hoped to get Jesus into similar trouble.

So Jesus was known to have strict views. If, then, in his saying about divorce and remarriage, he was merely siding with the influential school of Shammai, the disciples would hardly have been surprised. What surprised them was that he was even stricter than they imagined, even stricter than the stricter Jewish school. The only explanation for this is that they understood Jesus to be teaching (contrary to both Hillel and Shammai) that a divorcee should not remarry, even when the reason for divorce was the other partner's unfaithfulness.

Jesus does not correct their understanding. On the contrary, he goes on to teach that when one is divorced (the whole context is about divorce) it is right to 'renounce marriage' because of the demands of 'the kingdom of heaven' (v. 12). Jesus' reply (vv. 11 and 12) is discussed in greater detail in Chapter 8 of this book.

The second fact which convinces me is *Paul's quotation of Jesus' teaching*. In 1 Corinthians 7, Paul does what for him is unusual: he quotes the teaching of Jesus – 'To the married I give this command (not I but the Lord)' (v. 10). His quotation finishes at the end of verse 11, because verse 12 begins: 'To the rest I say this (I, not the Lord)'.

Verses 10 and 11 repeat Jesus' saying about divorce: 'A wife must not separate from her husband . . . And a husband must not divorce his wife.' In the middle comes this command: 'But if she does, she must remain unmarried or else be reconciled to her husband.'

Paul is used to issuing commands to the churches to which he writes. He is not one for saying, for example, 'Don't steal. But if, in disobedience to me, you do steal, then you must not benefit from the money you have stolen.' What to do as a second best, if you disobey his teaching, is not a subject Paul discusses.

But if Paul does not talk about what we might do if we choose to disobey him, it is inconceivable that when he is taking the rare step of quoting Christ's teaching (v. 10) and before he has even finished that teaching (v. 11b), he should interrupt Christ to say, 'But if you do disobey Christ, then, as a second best, you are to remain single or be reconciled to your partner.' That is a virtually impossible interpretation.

So what is Paul saying when he states: 'But if she does [divorce], she must remain unmarried or else be reconciled to her husband' (v. 11)? This is clearly an exception to Christ's teaching of no divorce (v. 10), and it is an exception which Paul mentions as part of his quotation of the teaching of Jesus (vv. 10-11; the quotation ends in v. 12). Jesus also gave one exception: divorce is permitted in the case of unfaithfulness (Matthew 5:32; 19:9).

The natural explanation, then, is this: Paul knew Christ's teaching in the form which Matthew preserves. He quotes Christ's teaching (vv. 10,11) and summarises it in this way: Christ said there was to be no divorce (vv. 10, 11b); Christ also, in his teaching, gave one exception and taught that if a woman (or man) takes advantage of that one legitimate exception, then she is 'to remain unmarried or else be reconciled to her husband' (v. 11a). That is the teaching of Christ which Paul passed on to the Corinthians: there is to be no remarriage, even in the exception to Christ's divorce teaching which Christ himself allowed.

So both the disciples' surprise and Paul's quotation of Jesus' teaching only really make sense on one understanding: Jesus in Matthew's Gospel teaches that 'God says no to divorce, except where there has been unfaithfulness, and no to remarriage under any circumstances, even where there has been unfaithfulness'.

What if my partner wasn't a Christian?

This was a situation apparently raised with Paul by the Corinthians and on which Christ had not specifically commented (1 Corinthians 7:12). It seems that there were a group of Christians at Corinth who thought that all sexual relations were suspect. The sentence 'It is well for a man not to touch a woman' (7:1, RSV) may well have been in their letter. If they believed that all sex, even between married couples, was wrong, it is understandable that they should be even more disturbed by marriage between a Christian and a non-Christian. So they almost certainly wrote to Paul asking whether they should divorce their non-Christian partners.

Paul quite clearly answers: no. 'If any brother has a wife who is not a believer and she is willing to live with him, he must not divorce her. And if a woman has a husband who is not a believer and he is willing to live with her, she must not divorce him' (vv. 12,13).

We saw earlier (Chapter 3) that what God does in marriage, he does for every couple. He joins every couple together as they marry, whether they believe in him or not. He makes every couple become, in his eyes, one flesh. Christian faith can enrich a marriage immeasurably, but the conversion of one partner, or the renunciation of Christian faith by one partner, does not affect the fact that God has joined them together and that they are one.

Of course the fact that one partner is a Christian and one is not can sometimes put great strains on a marriage. But Paul specifically says that it provides no grounds for divorce. If you are already legally divorced, the fact that your partner was not, and is not, a Christian gives no grounds for remarriage now.

What if my partner left me?

But what if my partner has deserted me? What if he ran off with another woman, or simply lost all commitment to the marriage and left?

Paul discusses what a Christian should do in these circumstances. He has in mind the specific situation which the Corinthians have raised: where a Christian is married to a non-Christian. He says, 'But if the unbeliever leaves, let him do so. A believing man or woman is not bound in such circumstances; God has called us to live in peace' (1 Corinthians 7:15).

Paul is answering a question about divorce. He has just said that a Christian must not divorce his (or her) non-Christian partner (vv. 12,13). If, however, the non-Christian partner leaves and wants a divorce, the Christian need not feel he or she must fight this tooth and nail; the Christian can agree to the divorce (v. 15).

It is probably legitimate to extend the application of this beyond the specific instance that Paul is being asked about. If my partner deserts me, for whatever reason, and presses me for a divorce, I need not feel that I have to refuse him or her. It is permitted, and often wisest, reluctantly to agree.

But am I then free to remarry? Some have argued that I am, on the grounds that Paul says, 'A believing man or woman is not bound in such circumstances' (v. 15). In fact Paul is not thinking of remarriage here at all. The word for 'bound' here means literally 'enslaved'; it is a completely different word from that used of the marriage bond in 7:39.

Paul has been asked a question about divorce. He says that we must never seek divorce (vv. 12,13) but we can agree to a divorce that our partner is wanting: 'If the unbeliever leaves, let him do so.' When Paul adds: 'A believing man or woman is not bound/

enslaved in such circumstances', he means that the Christian is not such a slave to remaining together as husband and wife that he or she must fight for it even against the other partner's wishes. The Christian is not *duty-bound* to continue with the marriage at all costs. That this is the meaning – you are not duty-bound to fight your partner against his or her will – is clear from the final statement in verse 15: 'God has called us to live in peace.'

So Paul is saying in verse 15 that a Christian may agree to a divorce which the partner who has deserted him wants. This is permissible; remarriage is not mentioned. Paul has already made clear whether remarriage is a moral possibility in the case of permitted divorce: 'she [he] must remain unmarried or else be reconciled to her husband [his wife]' (v. 11).

What if we weren't Christians when we married/divorced?

Lewis, whose story began this chapter, was not a Christian when he married; nor was his wife. Neither of them were Christians when they divorced. It was only in the aftermath of his divorce that Lewis became a Christian. Does this set him free to remarry? 2 Corinthians 5:17 is often quoted to support remarriage: 'If anyone is in Christ, he is a new creation; the old has gone, the new has come!'

This verse in 2 Corinthians, while tremendously important as a statement about new birth in Christ, was not written in a marriage context and has nothing directly to do with marriage. By contrast, 1 Corinthians 7:10-16 is specifically about marriage (it begins: 'To the married I give this command') and deals directly with the situation of how to view a marriage contracted before conversion.

In verses 12-16, Paul speaks about a marriage where one partner is a Christian and one is not. In view of the New Testament teaching that a Christian should only marry a fellow believer (7:39, compare 2 Corinthians 6:14–7:1), we may assume that in the majority of these marriages both were unbelievers when they married and one was subsequently converted. It seems that some Corinthians were feeling that their conversion nullified or dissolved (in God's eyes), or rendered unclean, their preconversion marriage to an unbeliever; they believed, therefore, that they should divorce their non-Christian partners.

Paul will have none of this (vv. 12-14). The Christian is just as much married to his non-Christian partner as he was before he became a Christian. Conversion should strengthen our commitment to our marriage vows, not weaken it. Even if we entered into marriage rashly and realise subsequently that it was a mistake, the Christian must consider himself bound by the vows that he has made (see Ecclesiastes 5:4-7).

But what if I am already not only married but divorced, and then become a Christian? To return to 2 Corinthians 5:17, Paul says that a Christian 'is a new creation; the old has gone, the new has come'. In context, this clearly means that God in Christ has dealt with our sin (we are 'reconciled to God' – v. 18) and with our selfishness (Christ 'died for all, that those who live should no longer live for themselves but for him who died for them and was raised again' – v. 15).

If we apply this to the divorced Christian, it brings the glorious news that Christ has forgiven me for any sin involved in my divorce and that Christ enables me to live for him, inspired by the sacrifice of his death and empowered by his resurrection life within me. Since Christ has said that the divorced Christian is not free to remarry because my original marriage still exists in God's eyes, becoming 'a new creation' means that I am able, in God's strength, to obey what he has commanded: to remain single or else be reconciled to my partner (1 Corinthians 7:11).

What if I'm already deeply involved with a divorcee?

Lewis and Janet were already in love and had seen a lot of each other, but they tried to get to grips with Christ's teaching before they went too far. What if a couple have gone a lot further? Suppose, for example, you are a divorced man and are already very deeply involved with a woman whom you had hoped to marry; or you are a woman who has never married and are engaged to a divorcee? You became involved thinking that God had nothing against such a relationship, and any early hesitations were silenced by the encouragement of your friends. But now that you are looking carefully at Christ's teaching, you are beginning to have serious doubts. Perhaps your doubts aren't shared by the person you love, and certainly you don't want to hurt him. What are you to do?

The first and most important question must be: am I free, under God, to marry this man (or woman)? The New Testament twice teaches specifically on the question of a proposed marriage where one partner is divorced. 'The man who marries a divorced woman commits adultery' (Luke 16:18); 'Whoever marries a divorced woman commits adultery' (Matthew 5:32, RSV). I have given reasons earlier in this chapter for believing that Christ ruled out such remarriage in all circumstances, including where there has been a divorce for unfaithfulness.

It is obviously extremely hard to put this teaching into practice if you have become deeply involved or even engaged. It will need a great deal of gentle, sensitive talking together. You will have to explain that you don't believe you are free to marry. You will need to ask forgiveness for the hurt you have caused and are causing, even though the last thing you wanted was to hurt someone you love deeply.

Breaking off any very close relationship is always painful. But we have to acknowledge that our first allegiance is to Christ, and so our attitude has to be the same as the apostles' when confronted with a tough choice: 'We must obey God rather than men' (Acts 5:29, compare 4:18,19).

And God is no man's debtor. Jesus said, 'If anyone loves me, he will obey my teaching. My Father will love him, and we will come to him and make our home with him . . . Peace I leave with you; my peace I give you. I do not give to you as the world gives. Do not let your hearts be troubled and do not be afraid' (John 14:23,27).

What if my partner has remarried?

When I made my marriage vow to my partner, I intended to keep it throughout my life. But now he has not only broken his vow; he has made it impossible to fulfil because he has remarried. Reconciliation between us is obviously out of the question. Am I not now finally free to remarry?

In the New Testament passage where the options open to the divorcee are unequivocally stated, only two options are given: 'If she does [divorce] she must remain unmarried or else be reconciled to her husband' (1 Corinthians 7:11). People sometimes say that remarriage is forbidden in order to leave open the possibility of reconciliation; if so, it would follow that where reconciliation is impossible remarriage can take place.

But in fact Paul does not say that she must remain single because of the possibility of reconciliation. And Jesus' own teaching (which Paul is quoting – see verse 10) makes it clear that she must remain single for quite a different reason. Remarriage for her would be 'adultery' (Matthew 5:32; 19:9; Mark 10:11,12; Luke 16:18) because she is still married to her first husband. He may have repudiated his vows, he may have gone off with another woman, but that does not mean that his divorced wife can follow suit and repudiate her marriage.

A man wrote to me recently: 'About nine years ago, my wife left me and married the pastor of our church, who was divorced from his wife about the same time. . . . From the start I took the approach that I could and should keep my marriage vow "till death do us part". After all, that is what I promised.'

It is not only our solemn promise that keeps us from remarrying. It is the recognition that God made us one with our partner; he joined us together; he formed the marriage bond.

And he has said that it is a bond which only death can free us from.

Do I really have to consider myself still married to my partner?

Supposing I have been very badly treated. My partner left me without any warning. He has said appalling lies about me in court, to my face and by letter. He has tried in every way to belittle me and to hurt me. He has poisoned the children against me. He has long since stopped any payments to support me or the children. I am so glad we are rid of him and want to have as little to do with him as possible. Do I really have to think that in God's eyes we are still married?

God does not ask us to continue living with such a person. At least where there has been persistent adultery, we are allowed to divorce our partner with God's approval (Matthew 5:32; 19:9). Divorce for adultery, which God permits, undoes the obligation to live together. But only death – not cruelty or unfaithfulness or even divorce – can undo the bond God created in marriage. 'A woman is bound to her husband as long as he lives. But if her husband dies, she is free to marry' (1 Corinthians 7:39).

Some parents abuse their children. If we are their children, we may need to have little or nothing to do with them. But we cannot undo the fact that they are our parents. Some husbands or wives abuse their marriage partner. After separation or divorce we may have little more to do with them, and they may want nothing more to do with us. But they remain the person we are married to. Many people experience this emotionally (it's far more difficult than one imagines to 'wash that man right out of my hair'), and this experience reflects the facts: God makes every couple one, in a bond which only death can undo.

So what does it mean in practice to consider myself still married to someone I now hate? *Positively,* it means to seek as much reconciliation as possible. As we shall see in Chapter 10, the Christian faith is all about reconciliation: God reconciling people to himself, God reconciling person to antagonised person. After divorce, the New Testament's preference is clearly that 'a wife . . . [may] be reconciled to her husband' (1 Corinthians 7:10,11) and a husband to his wife.

This does not necessarily mean that you will get back together again, but it does mean that you will seek to remove the hatred and bitterness from your reactions. Your anger in any case harms you far more than the partner you are angry with. Of course it takes two to make any real progress along the road of reconciliation, but you need to ask God to change you, so that you are more ready to understand, to forgive and to ask for forgiveness. You cannot simply wash your hands of this relationship; he/she remains the man/woman you are married to.

Negatively, this realisation means that you are not free to marry again. Since you are already married, you cannot marry anybody else. To do so would be to commit adultery, which is precisely what Jesus called a divorced person's second marriage.

What if everybody I know is encouraging me to remarry?

Everyone was encouraging Lewis and Janet to marry. It often happens from the earliest days after a husband and wife have separated. Our friends know we are depressed and hurt. They want to cheer us up. And so, without a thought about Christ's teaching on marriage nor about how many second marriages fail (far more than first marriages), especially if entered into in the early years after divorce, they say, 'You're good looking. There are plenty of women who'll be attracted to you'; 'You're still young. Go out and meet people. Anyone who married you would be a lucky man.'

Christians engage in this as much as anyone, often surreptitiously or quite openly seeking to engineer introductions and to matchmake. Normally Christians do this without thinking about the teaching of Jesus on remarriage or its implications for their friend's life. It is an area of Christ's teaching which most have simply blotted out of their minds. In fact, if they speak of it at all they tend to talk about 'what *the Church* teaches' as if Christ himself had been silent about remarriage.

If friends encourage us to remarry, gently but firmly we need to say, 'I don't want to. I don't believe it's right.' If their eyes respond: 'That's understandable at first; she'll come round to it,' we need to make it clear that Christ in his teaching has closed that door to us. It won't be helpful for them to keep suggesting some new relationship; we can do with all their help to remain true to Christ and to learn to be strong and contented in our new singleness.

Our friends, even some of our Christian friends, will be very surprised by this attitude, of course. So they were in Jesus' day. Jesus said, 'I tell you that anyone who divorces his wife, except for marital unfaithfulness, and marries another woman commits adultery' (Matthew 19:9). The disciples' reaction was one of utter amazement: 'If this is the situation between a husband and wife, it is better not to marry' (v. 10).

As we have seen (p. 97), the most natural explanation of this is that Jesus was distancing himself from the schools of Hillel (divorce and remarriage for any reason) and Shammai (divorce and remarriage only for sexual sin) by saying that there should be no remarriage under any circumstances. It caused consternation then; it causes consternation still today. But that is no reason for failing to obey the teaching of Christ which frequently, now as then, goes against received opinion.

Isn't it important for my children to have a loving man sharing their life?

The best environment for the healthy development of children is when they are able to live with their father and mother. Even when their parents have an icy relationship or are constantly at each other's throats, it is normally better for the children if the family can remain intact; and the children almost invariably perceive their parents' separation as a great loss.

If the parents have separated or divorced, it will help the children most in their development if they are able to keep in close touch with both father and mother. Their father remains enormously important to them and their psychological health. For the children to develop healthily, they need to have as easy a relationship with their father as possible and to see him frequently.

Where there has been a remarriage, the mother and her new husband may hope that their love will gradually replace the need for the biological father, so that he becomes relatively unimportant for the children's lives. This hope is rarely realised. The children may, or may not, in time develop a good relationship with their stepfather, but their father remains vitally important to them. One of Wallerstein and Kelly's principal findings is that even with remarriage and the increasing importance of a stepfather 'the biological father's emotional significance did not greatly diminish, although his influence on the daily life of children lessened'.[21]

Remarriage does frequently lessen the contact between father and children, to the detriment of their emotional development and psychological health. This is a reason why one or both parents often refrain from remarriage: to keep the children's relationship with their father strong.

But what if the father is completely out of the picture? What if he has long since ceased any contact with his children? Certainly it is important that all children, and especially boys, have good, close and healthy relationships with adult males; they need good male role models. These can, however, be provided by males other than a stepfather: by an uncle or uncle figure, or by a youth group leader. These relationships can be extremely important and nurturing.

Remarriage, on the other hand, is often seen by the children as disruptive, and frequently – at least in the early stages and often for much longer – adds to their turmoil. When asked why she had not remarried, a woman in our church replied: 'My children were my priority, and by this time I had heard of so many situations where the children were in the middle and either unable to accept a new stepfather or, worse, the new partner was unable to accept the children.'

Of course there is enormous loss for the children in the father's leaving. There is still more when the father dies. But the answer is not always, in either situation, for the mother to remarry. It may be better for the mother to encourage strong relationships with other adult males, especially if God has said no to remarriage after divorce.

What if I am desperately lonely?

Loneliness is one of the deepest pains of divorce. As I write, I have just been speaking to a man whose wife left him only a few days ago; he sees 'years of loneliness stretching before me'.

Men sometimes feel that at least their wife has the children, and friends at the school gate and in the church to support her, whereas they are at work all day and too exhausted and emotionally drained to do anything in the evening. Women often feel that their husband can go where he likes and do what he wants whereas they are stuck in the home, cooped up with the children, not able to get baby-sitters because they can't afford them and because, being on their own, they're no longer able to take part in a baby-sitting circle. When loneliness is so acute, isn't marrying again – or at least starting a new relationship – the answer?

Even if Christ hadn't forbidden remarriage after divorce, the answer would probably be no. Intense feelings of loneliness are very often a sign that we are not yet ready emotionally for a new relationship. And many, many divorcees take on a new relationship too early – whether marriage, or a partner living in, or just an exclusive male-female friendship – with disastrous results. They want to assuage their loneliness but they are not yet sufficiently healed to form a stable relationship, and the result in the large majority of cases is a fresh breakup and further pain.

But in any case, Christ taught that in his eyes the original marriage still exists and that remarriage is, therefore, not an option. Does that mean that God has just left us to cope as best we can with our loneliness, that he doesn't care? On the contrary, God cares especially for the lonely and provides for their needs: 'God sets the lonely in families, he leads forth the prisoners with singing' (Psalm 68:6). God does not intend us to be alone. He gives us warm, supportive friendships and sets us free from the prison of our loneliness and self-pity.

Of course his great desire is to see us reconciled to our marriage partner. Where that is not possible, the Christian is denied the possibility of a further husband or wife. But by contrast the Christian is given an entirely new family to offer support and comfort and to provide the loving relationships we need.

Jesus was once told that his human family was looking for him. He replied, 'Here are my mother and my brothers! Whoever does God's will is my brother and sister and mother' (Mark 3:31-35). Many divorcees have found not only that they have been able to survive the worst times thanks to their Christian family, but that their loneliness has largely disappeared because of the rich friendships that God has given them.

It is very important, therefore, that you don't withdraw from Christian friendships or from involvement in the family of the Church. You may feel awkward at first, but these are the very people – your brothers and sisters – whom God has provided to help, love and support you in your loneliness.

What if the only real alternative is my living with another man/woman?

Sexual urges are strong. The first man who ever spoke to me about his divorce said, 'The hardest thing is not being able to have sex.' A woman who wrote to me recently is typical of many: 'I found the ending of sexual life much harder than I'd expected. Although it wasn't marvellous, nineteen years is a long time to establish habits that are abruptly ceased.'

So isn't it 'better to marry than to burn with passion' (1 Corinthians 7:9), especially if the only realistic alternative is to live with a new partner without marrying? Paul of course is not talking about divorcees in the verse just quoted, but to 'the unmarried and the widows' (vv. 8,9). Two verses later he does tell the divorced what they must do: 'remain unmarried or else be reconciled to her husband [his wife]' (v. 11). So his authority cannot be used to sanction remarriage when sexual passions are strong.

We live in an age which wants to deny responsibility, especially where sexual practice is concerned: 'I can't help it', 'My feelings get the better of me', 'I'm only in my twenties and I can't be expected to remain sexually inactive for the rest of my life'.

The Bible certainly teaches that the sex drive is strong and even devotes an entire book, the Song of Songs, to the celebration of romantic and sexual love. But it is equally and repeatedly clear that sexual play must only take place within marriage and that sex outside marriage is forbidden.

Moreover, our sexual urges are not beyond our control: 'No temptation has seized you except what is common to man. And God is faithful; he will not let you be tempted beyond what you can bear. But when you are tempted, he will also provide a way out so that you can stand up under it' (1 Corinthians 10:13).

That 'way out' will not be remarriage. He will not relieve you of the temptation to do one thing he has forbidden (sleeping with someone to whom you're not married) by guiding you into something else he has forbidden (remarriage after divorce). Rather, he will give you the grace to control your sexual desires and remain pure: 'My grace is sufficient for you, for my power is made perfect in weakness' (2 Corinthians 12:9).

What about my sense of failure which a good second marriage would heal?

A deep sense of failure almost always accompanies divorce. There is nothing more devastating than to hear the person that (at least at some point) you have loved most in the world saying: I no longer love you or need you. One woman wrote of her experience: 'Emotionally I felt shell-shocked. I was a failure. If I hadn't been able to keep my husband, what hope did I have? I swung from unnatural highs to the deepest lows.'

This sense of failure needs to be healed; self-confidence needs gradually to be restored. Many divorcees find that healing does begin to come as they make a success of some other area of their life: women go back into the full-time workforce and find they do well in a responsible job; men sometimes find they are becoming much better and more thoughtful fathers; men and women often come for the first time to know Christ through their divorce or deepen their life with him. Perhaps they experience God using them to help other people, especially those who are going through deep pain themselves.

Most importantly, healing comes with understanding: gradually coming to see more clearly why the marriage broke down, accepting your part in its problems, asking for and receiving forgiveness from God and, if possible, your partner, and grasping even more deeply the truth that God loves us and wholeheartedly accepts us.

It is true that a second marriage can also help in confidence being restored, although even a good second marriage will only bring partial healing. The scars will always be with you; even happily married divorcees normally carry some sense of failure with them for the rest of their life.

But remarriage is not the only way to find healing, and we must in any case look for healing to come in God's way, by God's permitted means. And he will heal: 'The Lord lifts up those who are bowed down' (Psalm 146:8). 'Thou, O Lord, art a shield about me, my glory, and the lifter of my head' (Psalm 3:3, RSV). Craigie comments on this last verse: 'The lifting of the head signifies the move from despair to hope.'[22] God will restore our self-confidence and our hope, if we let him.

What happens if I disobey Christ's teaching?

What happens if I know that it's wrong in Christ's eyes to remarry, but I go ahead – or have gone ahead – anyway?

Christians can ask this question at two very different stages. They can ask it *before* they decide finally whether or not to get married a second time, or they can ask it *after* they have remarried, now seeing that they disobeyed Christ's teaching whereas at the time they had not understood Christ's prohib-ition and believed they were doing the right thing.

Of course it can be an agonising question to face, perhaps especially before a final decision. You may be very much in love, you want desperately to get married, but you are largely convinced that in Christ's eyes your marrying again would be 'adultery'. In the end, it must boil down to who has your first love and your first allegiance. Christ said that the greatest command is to 'love the Lord your God with all your heart and with all your soul and with all your mind and with all your strength' (Mark 12:28-31; Matthew 22:34-40; compare Luke 10:25-28). He also said that this love must be worked out into practical obedience: 'If you love me, you will obey what I command' (John 14:15; compare vv. 21,23).

It may be hard at the moment to echo John's words: 'This is love for God: to obey his commands. And his commands are not burdensome' (1 John 5:3; compare Matthew 11:29,30). Never-theless, as we give ourselves to growing in love for God, other loves and other desires will become less important. We will be able to sing with increasing sincerity the words of a contemporary worship song: 'The greatest thing in all my life is knowing you.'

But the question: 'What if I disobey Christ's teaching?' can be asked from a very different perspective. Some may ask it who have remarried and now come to see that they were going against the teaching of Christ in marrying a second time. How does Christ see them now? Can they ever be forgiven?

They not only can be forgiven, but – as with any other act of disobedience – they have been forgiven immediately they acknowledged their fault. Speaking of sexual sins, Paul can say, 'Do you not know that the wicked will not inherit the kingdom of God? Do not be deceived: neither the sexually immoral nor idolaters nor adulterers nor male prostitutes nor homosexual offenders . . . will inherit the kingdom of God. And that is what some of you were. But you were washed, you were sanctified, you were justified in the name of the Lord Jesus Christ and by the Spirit of our God' (1 Corinthians 6:9-11).

Paul includes in that list 'adulterers'. He was doubtless thinking of those who, while married both legally and in the eyes of God, had sexual intercourse outside marriage. If such people, when repentant, can be wholly forgiven, we can be quite sure that the Christian who entered a second marriage believing he was doing what was right but now sees that he was inadvertently disobeying Christ's teaching has been 'washed . . . sanctified . . . [and] justified in the name of our Lord Jesus Christ and by the Spirit of our God'. Where there is sorrow for past error and blindness, any guilt or sin has been wholly forgiven.

How does God view the second marriage I'm in?

It may be reassuring to know that God has forgiven any disobedience in my marrying again, though some will find it hard emotionally to accept as disobedience a wedding that has brought them great joy. But isn't the logic of Christ's position that we are now 'living in sin' and that God sees us as being in a continuing adulterous relationship?

No. God views your new married relationship primarily as a marriage; as a marriage which should not have been entered into, as a mistake, but nevertheless as a true marriage. We can see this very clearly by analogy. The Bible teaches that a Christian should only marry another Christian. The Old Testament states repeatedly that a member of the people of God should only marry another member (e.g. Deuteronomy 7:1-4; Ezra 9:1-2). This is reaffirmed in the teaching of the New Testament (1 Corinthians 7:39; compare 2 Corinthians 6:14–7:1).

If a Christian nevertheless goes ahead and marries someone who is not a Christian, this is an act of disobedience; it is breaking a command of God. But it is still a marriage that has been entered into, and a marriage that is to be respected. The marriages between Christians and non-Christians which Paul discusses in 1 Corinthians 7:12-16 must surely include cases where someone who is already a Christian marries an unbeliever, and Paul's categorical command is that the marriage should be fully supported and that there should be no divorce (vv. 12-14).

A further, and still closer, analogy is with polygamy. The Christian view is that no person should be married to more than one other at any time. 1 Timothy 3:2,12 and Titus 1:6 certainly include a prohibition of polygamy, although their meaning in context is probably more narrowly defined.[23]

In some societies, however, men have several wives (and in others, women have several husbands). Missionaries and church councils have generally taken the view that these second and third marriages, while they should not have been entered into, should nevertheless be treated as full marriages and should be respected and supported.

It is entirely in keeping with this understanding to say that a second marriage after divorce should not have been contracted and yet must now be recognised as a marriage and be given the same support as any other marriage.

To be more specific: in polygamous societies, Christians have normally taught that existing polygamous marriages should be respected and upheld (see Exodus 21:10; Deuteronomy 21:15-17), but that all further requests for a second or third marriage should be forbidden. So, in our society which allows for and encourages remarriage while a divorced partner is still living, Christians can with consistency (although with sadness) accept and respect existing remarriages after divorce but can teach against, and refuse to perform, any new marriage of a divorcee.

What if God has clearly been blessing my new marriage?

I can understand the argument that Christ says my first marriage still exists despite our legal divorce and that therefore I shouldn't have entered a second marriage. But if that were true, surely my second marriage would be a disaster? In reality, I experience the exact opposite. It has brought enormous happiness to me, to my new partner, to my children, to us as a couple together in the service of God. So can it really have been wrong?

Of course there are many second marriages which bring great happiness to all those most closely involved. We have to acknowledge, however, that this is not the norm. Most second marriages end in divorce (considerably more than first marriages)[24] and most second marriages prove more difficult than first marriages, especially where children are involved.

Nevertheless, some second marriages are very clearly and richly blessed by God. What does this prove? It proves one thing and one thing only: that God is very gracious. It cannot prove that remarriage is right in God's eyes; that question must be decided not by individual experience but by examining the teaching of the Bible (see Chapter 2).

James reminds us that 'we all make many mistakes' (James 3:2, RSV). We make some without realising what we have done; we make some deliberately. But in neither case does God write us off. Samson made some disastrous mistakes, especially in the women he married or slept with (Judges 14; 16:1,4-22), yet this did not stop the Lord using him and even using his marriages (see especially 14:3,4).

Of course there is much good in your second marriage. If God can bless Samson's marriages, he will certainly bless yours. The companionship and love you give each other, the ways you are able to serve others in your home and in the church, are only some of the signs of God's goodness to you as a couple. Of course now that you are married God is committed to that new relationship and blesses and strengthens it.

I have a very close Christian friend who married a Muslim. He agonised over the decision and knew really that he was disobeying Christ in marrying someone who was not a Christian. Now, twenty years on, God has given them both a remarkably strong, happy marriage, though his wife is still a Muslim. He should not have married her, but he is certainly right not only to rejoice in his wife but to acknowledge God's continual blessing of their marriage.

God in his grace blesses marriages that, if we had listened to him, we would not have embarked on.

Is Christ saying that I should leave my second marriage and go back to my first?

Emphatically no. In the Old Testament there is only one law which deals in any detail with divorce (Deuteronomy 24:1-4). It is not easy to understand every aspect of the law, but it envisages a situation in which a man has divorced, remarried and then subsequently wants to return to his first wife. It categorically forbids this.

If you have remarried after divorce, you have made very solemn vows to your new husband or wife. If you had understood and followed Christ's teaching about marriage, you would not have made these vows; but you have.

You are now, as we have seen already, in a similar situation to a Christian who, in ignorance of Christ's teaching or known disobedience to it, has married an unbeliever. The Corinthians were concerned that such a mixed marriage would render them 'unclean' or 'unholy' in God's eyes (see 1 Corinthians 7:14). But Paul reassured them: they are not defiled by their marriage; rather the marriage of a Christian makes God look more favourably on her husband/his wife and their children (1 Corinthians 7:14).

Similarly, you need not feel that your marriage is 'unclean' or 'unholy' in God's eyes. On the contrary, he upholds the decision you have made and looks favourably on your family. It may be possible for you to forgive your first partner and achieve some measure of reconciliation with him (see Chapter 10), but it would be entirely contrary to God's will for you to repudiate the new marriage vows you have made and return to live with your first partner. Vows, even mistaken vows, are to be kept (see Ecclesiastes 5:4-7).

Can I trust God and not begin a new relationship?

It is often hard to trust anyone after your marriage has broken up. The person you once thought you could trust entirely has let you down. And that frequently destroys any trust: in people you meet, in friends, in anyone offering friendship or help. So when God tells you that you're not to begin a new romantic or sexual relationship, can you really trust him to meet your deepest needs and to give you a full and satisfying life?

It is a fundamental fact about God that he is faithful, that he can be trusted: 'The Lord is faithful to all his promises and loving towards all he has made. The Lord upholds all those who fall and lifts up all who are bowed down' (Psalm 145:13,14). In fact the Bible repeatedly affirms the faithfulness of God, perhaps most famously in Lamentations 3:22-24 – 'The steadfast love of the Lord never ceases, his mercies never come to an end; they are new every morning; great is thy faithfulness. "The Lord is my portion," says my soul, "therefore I will hope in him"' (RSV).

But the Bible also asserts that God's faithfulness is primarily shown to 'those who love him and keep his commands'

(Deuteronomy 7:9). This is most succinctly put in the phrase 'To the faithful you show yourself faithful' (2 Samuel 22:26; Psalm 18:25). We cannot expect to disobey God and then find him fulfilling his promises to us. But if we steadfastly determine to remain obedient to him, we will find him utterly reliable in all the good that he promises us.

He asks us to give up a lot, and he also promises much. Simon Peter said to Jesus, 'We have left all we had to follow you!' And Jesus replied, 'I tell you the truth, no-one who has left home or wife or brothers or parents or children for the sake of the kingdom of God will fail to receive many times as much in this age [the parallel passage in Mark says: 'a hundred times as much in this present age'] and, in the age to come, eternal life' (Luke 18:28-30; Mark 10:28-30).

Many divorced Christians have deliberately given up all thought of living with a new wife or husband and family 'for the sake of the kingdom of God' and have proved in their own experience the consistent faithfulness and enriching love of God.

Key verses

'Fear the Lord, you his saints, for those who fear him lack nothing . . . Those who seek the Lord lack no good thing' (Psalm 34:9,10).

CHAPTER 8

QUESTIONS ABOUT SINGLENESS HAVING BEEN MARRIED

Kate had always wanted to be married. As a child, she had loved dressing up in anything lacy or silky and playing at 'weddings' with her sisters. The highlight of her preschool years had been when she was a bridesmaid to her godmother, and afterwards she had worn that bridesmaid's dress until it was grubby and tattered.

She married Ian when she was twenty-three and was pregnant only a few months later. Three years after Simon was born, they had a daughter Elizabeth.

Kate thought that her marriage was fairly normal: it had its rough patches, but overall it was good and satisfying. But then, when Simon was twelve and Elizabeth nine, the relationship began to deteriorate. Work was increasingly taking Ian away from home, and when he was with the family he was strangely absent-minded. After six months, Kate began to have her suspicions. Eventually she asked him point blank whether he was having an affair. All the rather sordid details came out. The following weekend, Ian collected his things and left.

Kate joined a support group for the separated and divorced. There she met Moira whose husband had left her thirty years earlier with children aged seven, five and two. Moira had never remarried, and Kate was full of questions about how Moira had found being single after her divorce and how she had managed to bring up three children on her own.

What are the advantages of being single after separation/divorce?

There are advantages to being single again. Initially many people feel relief. There have often been months of uncertainty with a lot of talk (or thinking about) separation, and at last the decision has been taken. Another immediate cause of relief may be that all the tension and conflict has gone from the home. One husband said, 'This is the first week of peace I've had in years.' A wife wrote, 'After a horrific previous eighteen months, and years of unhappiness, it was in a way a great relief to be alone.'

Another immediate advantage can be a considerable sense of freedom: I can cook what I like, be the person I choose, do what I want. I am no longer tied to a person who cramps me and wants to dictate to me at every turn.

After the initial relief, the disadvantages of separation often become clearer. It is then that people who have had high hopes of the good which separation will accomplish frequently crash into depression.

But as the months and then years go on, further advantages of being single become apparent. Some of these are related to achievements, which can do a great deal to restore and enhance one's self-esteem. In most marriages the jobs are parcelled out: one partner deals with the finances, one washes and irons, one is more involved in the children's schooling, one may be the decision-taker, one plans the holidays. The other partner may have begun to feel that he (or she) couldn't handle those things. It can be very healthy to grow in independence and to know that you can handle almost any aspect of personal or family life.

This sense of achievement can also come in other ways: by having to go back into part or full-time work and finding you are able to do well in a responsible job; by determining to go out and contribute to the community through voluntary work; by making a greater success of being a parent; by developing interests which your partner never allowed or encouraged.

Many find that divorce plunges them into an identity crisis: who am I, now that people no longer think of me as Ian's wife? But over a period of time it becomes clear who I really am, now that Ian is no longer forcing me into the mould he has chosen for me. That can be a tremendous gain.

Above all, many divorcees are able to find God precisely because they no longer have anyone else to rely upon. Tom Jones traces his progress in reacting to being alone. After two or three years, he found that being on his own had become 'a new opportunity to discover myself and to take positive new directions in life. My aloneness [became] my teacher . . . I came to experience a much deeper and more personal relationship with God than I had ever known before'.[25]

Often divorcees come to echo the words of Psalm 119:71 – 'It was good for me to be afflicted so that I might learn your decrees.' Divorce has been a desperately unhappy experience, but they would never have come to know God so deeply and personally without it.

What are the disadvantages of being single after separation/divorce?

The disadvantages are also many and deeply painful. For most people the greatest disadvantage is loneliness, felt especially acutely when there is nothing else to do: at some meal-times, in the evenings, in bed. There is no one to share with, no one to talk to, no one with whom to discuss the decisions. There is no one to cuddle, no one with whom to have sex.

There are normally great losses associated with children. Some divorcees who have no children and who believe they should not remarry or don't think they will remarry mourn the fact that they will never have children. Fathers often feel acutely the loss of their children. Mothers may crave adult company and a break from the children and home.

Money almost always proves a problem. Both partners are likely to be substantially worse off, having to curtail drastically the lifestyle they've become accustomed to; and the wives are normally hit harder financially.

All this can be exacerbated by self-pity. Psalm 73 is about a man who became bitter because he was the one who had stayed true to God but he believed God had let him down: 'I envied the arrogant when I saw the prosperity of the wicked. They have no struggles . . . The evil conceits of their minds know no limits. They scoff, and speak with malice. . . . This is what the wicked are like – always carefree, they increase in wealth. Surely in vain have I kept my heart pure; in vain have I washed my hands in innocence. All day long I have been plagued; I have been punished every morning' (Psalm 73:3-14).

But then he sees that this kind of thinking and talking is actually a distortion (v. 15) and he begins to get his perspective back when he comes close to God (vv. 16,17). 'When my heart was grieved and my spirit embittered, I was senseless and ignorant; I was a brute beast before you. Yet I am always with you; you hold me by my right hand' (vv. 21-23).

What does God say about the single life?

To many people, even those who have been Christians for a long time, what the New Testament says about being single is very surprising. Our society tends to see singleness – having no marital, or at least sexual, relationship – in an almost totally negative light. Christians often feel very sorry for those who are not married. And so did the Jews of Jesus' day. An early Jewish commentary on Genesis states: 'Whoever has no wife lives without good, without help, without joy, without blessing, without atonement' (Genesis Rabbah 17:2). The Talmud pronounces: 'Any man who has no wife is no proper man' (*b. Yeb.* 63a).

Yet the New Testament has a totally different attitude to the single life, revolutionary for its own day, revolutionary for ours. 1 Corinthians 7 has the longest passage of teaching on singleness in the New Testament. Here, towards the beginning of the chapter, singleness is called a 'gift from God' (v. 7). Jesus teaches precisely the same. He speaks of singleness as a life that 'has been given' by God to some (Matthew 19:11).

It is a gift which is to be desired and cherished. Though Paul of course recognises that marriage is God's will for many, he says, 'I wish that all men were as I am'; that is, single (1 Corinthians 7:7). Paul may, incidentally, have known both singleness and marriage, since with his strict Jewish education (Acts 22:3) it is very likely that he had been married and was now either a widower or divorced. It is well known that some of the finest teaching exalting marriage comes in Paul's epistles (e.g. Ephesians 5:21-33). But Paul speaks just as highly, or even more highly (1 Corinthians 7:38), of the single life; and he does so for three reasons.

First, he is *realistic about marriage*. He says that 'those who marry will face many troubles in this life' and remaining single 'spare[s] you this' (1 Corinthians 7:28). It is perhaps understandable that those who have never married should have an unrealistic, idealised picture of marriage. When I interview engaged couples, they almost all tell me that they know each other thoroughly and that they either never have rows or put them completely aside within a few hours. It is more surprising that those who have been married and have known the pain of separation should fall for the same deception when they find themselves in love again. But Paul is more realistic. Of course there are pains and difficulties in being single, but there are quite as many in being married.

Second, he is *forward looking*. He is not under a further illusion: that our existence on earth is all there is to life. On the contrary, his whole outlook is controlled by the fact that 'this world in its present form is passing away' (v. 31), that Christ is coming again and that we must be as little tied to this world as possible (vv. 29-31). Jesus had earlier taught that 'the people of this age marry and are given in marriage. But those who are considered worthy of taking part in that age and in the resurrection from the dead will neither marry nor be given in marriage' (Luke 20:34,35). In heaven there will be no marriage. It is entirely in keeping with this for Paul to say both that the married should not act as if their marriage was all important and eternal (1 Corinthians 7:29) and that, in the light of eternity, singleness now may be preferable as it ties us less to this world (vv. 25-31).

Third, he *desires complete devotion to the Lord.* This is such an important part of his teaching that it is worth quoting in full:

> [32]An unmarried man is concerned about the Lord's affairs – how he can please the Lord. [33]But a married man is concerned about the affairs of this world – how he can please his wife – [34]and his interests are divided. An unmarried woman or virgin is concerned about the Lord's affairs: Her aim is to be devoted to the Lord in both body and spirit. But a married woman is concerned about the affairs of this world – how she can please her husband. [35]I am saying this for your own good, not to restrict you, but that you may live in a right way in undivided devotion to the Lord. (1 Corinthians 7:32-35)

This teaching is very clear. Married people, of necessity and rightly, are anxious to please other people and to satisfy those people's needs and desires: first and foremost their marriage partner's (vv. 33,34) and then later their children's as well. They cannot be wholeheartedly or 'undividedly' taken up with pleasing the Lord (vv. 32,34), growing in holiness (v. 34 reads literally: 'that she may be holy both in body and spirit') and living in utter devotion to the Lord (v. 35). The unmarried, by contrast, are able to live in much more single-minded love for the Lord.

This is manifestly true in experience. Rhena Taylor writes: 'There can be no denying that the single person can offer his or her life more freely to the Lord . . . and so, perhaps, has a greater opportunity both to "suffer for his sake" and to know a very special relationship with him.'[26] In many churches those who are most respected for their love of Christ and their lives of prayer and Christian service are single members of the Church family.

This teaching in 1 Corinthians 7 about the great benefits of the Christian single life is addressed primarily to 'virgins' (v. 25), which may in context mean those who are engaged but certainly refers to those who have never been married. But since this teaching comes shortly after what Paul has said about divorce and his quotation of Jesus: 'If she does [divorce], she must remain unmarried or else be reconciled to her husband' (v. 11), his words clearly apply to the single divorcee as well. He shows not only that a divorcee must remain unmarried (or better still: be reconciled to his/her partner) (v. 11), but that there are enormous benefits, especially spiritual benefits, in the single life. Of course these promised benefits are not automatic; they only become reality when single Christians accept them fully and make the most of them.

There is an even closer connection between divorce and teaching about singleness in Christ's words in Matthew 19. As we have seen before, Jesus is asked a question about divorce (v. 3). His final answer to the Pharisees comes in verse 9, which principally responds to their question about divorce but also for the first time introduces the question of remarriage: 'I tell you that anyone who divorces his wife, except for marital unfaithfulness, and marries another woman commits adultery' (v. 9).

It is this prohibition of remarriage after legitimate divorce which so astonishes the disciples. And so they exclaim, 'If this is the situation between a husband and wife, it is better not to marry' (v. 10). They are probably deliberately overstating their case; they know perfectly well that Jesus is not suggesting that first marriages are prohibited or unwise. The disciples probably hope that he will soften his teaching against remarriage after divorce.

But if so, they are disappointed. Jesus teaches instead about singleness and distinguishes three types of people who either are not able to marry or should not contemplate marriage: 'Some are eunuchs because they were born that way; others were made that way by men; and others have renounced marriage [literally: made themselves eunuchs] because of the kingdom of heaven' (v. 12). Some then, perhaps for a variety of reasons, are not made (from birth) for marriage; others, again perhaps in a variety of ways, have been rendered incapable of marriage because of what other people have done to them; and a third group have voluntarily renounced any thought of marriage because they know this is what obedience to God ('the kingdom of heaven') demands.

It is quite clear that Jesus is principally teaching about this third group, to whom singleness has been 'given' by God (v. 11; compare 1 Corinthians 7:7). It is equally clear from the entire context (vv. 3-12) that Jesus is principally concerned with those who have been through a divorce. It is they who are to 'renounce marriage because of the kingdom of heaven' (v. 12).

Didn't God say, 'It is not good for a man (or woman) to be alone'?

But if God has such a high view of the single life, isn't he contradicting himself? In Genesis 2:18 he says, 'It is not good for the man to be alone. I will make a helper suitable for him.' The animals wouldn't do (vv. 19,20) and God provided marriage as the answer to the universal human need for companionship and mutual support.

Genesis 2 does indeed show that loneliness is not God's will for anyone and that his principal answer for most people is a husband or wife. Even for these people, however, marriage is not

God's only provision for loneliness. Many contemporary husbands and wives expect their partners to provide in its entirety the support and encouragement they need, and under the strain of these unrealistic expectations marriages frequently crack.

But in any case marriage is not God's way of giving companionship to everyone. Jesus was never married; Paul was certainly single by the time he wrote; and those who have been through divorce are to 'remain unmarried or else be reconciled' to their partner (1 Corinthians 7:11). If God knows that it is also not good for these people to be alone (see Genesis 2:18), how does he provide for their needs? One answer, the most important human answer, is through *friends*. Christians in their desire to promote marriage are often guilty of devaluing friendship.

A typical example is the treatment of Ecclesiastes 4:9-12 – 'Two are better than one, because they have a good return for their work: If one falls down, his friend can help him up. . . . Though one may be overpowered, two can defend themselves. A cord of three strands is not quickly broken.' This is frequently used as the text for a wedding sermon to show the value of marital companionship, especially where Jesus is also included ('a cord of three strands'). But despite the mention of keeping warm together on a cold night (v. 11), this is not about marriage at all, but about friendship ('his friend', [v. 10]). The passage says how good it is to have one close friend, so that you can help each other (v. 10) and protect each other (v. 12); and better still to have two close friends (v. 12).

In the early months after the breakup of their marriage, people often make one of two mistakes. They either hide away from all relationships because they feel that they can never trust anyone again or they plunge into a new sexual or marital relationship for which they are not emotionally ready even if God had permitted it. What they need instead is good, reliable friendships, especially with those of their own sex, and with people who, like Jonathan with David when he was in deep trouble, can 'strengthen their hands in God' (see 1 Samuel 23:16, RSV).

God's other great provision is *himself.* When Adam was lonely, God sought for him a 'helper' (Genesis 2:18). The same Hebrew word is used again and again in the Old Testament of God himself. Perhaps the most famous example is Psalm 121, 'I lift up my eyes to the hills – where does my help come from? My help comes from the Lord, the Maker of heaven and earth' (Psalm 121:1,2; compare Psalm 46:1). A less familiar verse is particularly apt for those who are the 'victims' of divorce or who are looking after children whose father has left them: 'You, O God, do see trouble and grief; you consider it to take it in hand. The victim commits himself to you; you are the helper of the fatherless' (Psalm 10:14). Many divorcees have found that the friendship of Christ has become the richest relationship they have ever known and the deepest (although, again, not the only) answer to their loneliness.

What if I just can't accept Christ's teaching?

When the disciples said that it might be better for a couple not to marry, Jesus replied, 'Not everyone can accept this word, but only those to whom it has been given' (Matthew 19:11). He then gave his teaching about those who 'renounce marriage because of the kingdom of heaven' and added: 'The one who can accept this should accept it' (v. 12). So what if I can't accept it? What if I feel very differently about singleness from what I read in 1 Corinthians 7? What if I am the kind of person who simply feels incomplete without marriage, who feels that 'I've been made for marriage'?

It's important to understand what Jesus is saying in Matthew 19. He is not saying, 'Here is my advice; you can accept it or ignore it. You can take it or leave it.' The word Jesus uses here (NIV: 'accept') means 'to grasp with a view to acting on it'.[27] Almost all commentators say this is the exact equivalent of Jesus' frequent expression: 'He who has ears (to hear), let him hear' (e.g. Matthew 11:15). It is, therefore, not an invitation to refuse God's call to the divorced to 'renounce marriage', but a challenge to obey.

Indeed it is vital that you do accept your single life. Jones warns how damaging it can be to rebel against singleness, saying, 'I *will not* accept this . . . I am *going* to be married again.' He comments: 'If you are . . . single, to rebel against singleness is to rebel against your life and, ultimately, to rebel against God . . . So accept where you are and do everything that you can to make your life positive, healthy and enjoyable.'[28]

Margaret Evening gives the same warning that 'non-acceptance leads to bitterness and self-pity, both of which are most unattractive and ultimately destructive', and she quotes Michel Quoist's poem about a celibate priest who pours out to God his intense feelings of loneliness at the end of a busy Sunday. The poem ends:

> Son, you are not alone.
> I am with you . . .
> Lord tonight, while all is still and I feel sharply
>   the sting of solitude, . . .
> While the whole world presses on my shoulders
>   with all its weight of misery and sin,
> I repeat to you my 'yes' – not in a burst of laughter,
>   but slowly, clearly, humbly,
> Alone Lord, before you,
> In the peace of the evening.[29]

What if being single makes me the very opposite of 'holy' and 'devoted to the Lord'?

It's all very well for Paul to say that one of the great advantages of being single is that I can be more 'holy in body and spirit' (1 Corinthians 7:34, RSV) and can 'live . . . in undivided devotion to the Lord' (1 Corinthians 7:35). But what if the effect on me is the exact reverse? What if I find that having to be single again after my divorce makes me angry, often fills me with self-pity and generally makes me more taken up with me and my needs? What if I feel strongly that I would be considerably more 'holy' and certainly more 'devoted to the Lord' if he allowed me a new marriage?

There is of course real force in this argument. Paul is certainly not saying that the single life automatically leads to greater holiness and devotion to the Lord. He is saying that it provides an opportunity for this greater closeness to Christ. Whether that becomes a reality must depend on how much we are willing to accept God's will for us.

The answer to this question must be the same as in any area where our instinctive reaction is to rebel against what God is asking of us. We are not free, as Christians, to give in to our rebellious instinct and reject God's teaching; rather we are to ask God to change our negative attitude.

And that will take time. We need to be patient with ourselves; we need to be patient with God: 'I waited patiently for the Lord; he turned to me and heard my cry. He lifted me out of the slimy pit, out of the mud and mire; he set my feet on a rock and gave me a firm place to stand. He put a new song in my mouth, a hymn of praise to our God. Many will see and fear and put their trust in the Lord' (Psalm 40:1-3). We must ask God for help not merely to put up with our singleness (to be 'lifted out of the slimy pit') but to feel positively about it ('a new song in my mouth') and to use our welcome of the single life to help others ('many will see and fear and put their trust in the Lord'). This change in us will come gradually, as we 'wait patiently for the Lord'.

What about my sexual needs?

For many, the sexual drive is very strong. It is difficult enough for anyone to remain sexually pure in our society, which is so saturated with images of sex and scornful of anyone who aims to live without sexual activity. The desire for sexual play and sexual intercourse is often stronger in the divorced who have got used to regular, satisfying sex in marriage, often right up to, and frequently after, the breakup. Since the Bible forbids extramarital sex, isn't it both wrong and harmful to deny a legitimate outlet for our sexual needs by prohibiting remarriage?

The Bible acknowledges that our sexual instincts are strong and are given by God. It also recognises that in some the sexual urge is particularly powerful and that this may be one good reason for entering a first marriage (1 Corinthians 7:36, RSV). But it certainly does not say that human beings have a need for sexual intercourse which *must* be satisfied. C. S. Lewis is typically clear: 'The Christian rule is: "Either marriage, with complete faithfulness to your partner, or else total abstinence." Now this is so difficult, and so contrary to our instincts, that obviously either Christianity is wrong or our sexual instinct, as it now is, has gone wrong. One or the other . . . I think it is the instinct which has gone wrong.'[30]

The divorcee is, in God's eyes and therefore in reality, still married to his or her original partner. Sex with that marriage partner has normally become impossible, yet what Lewis calls the sexual instinct is still very much present. Since, then, the sexual urge is still very strong but it has no legitimate outlet, it needs not to be indulged – whether on our own, through pornographic literature and film, or with others, through a temporary or permanent sexual relationship – but to be controlled; and that is only possible with God's help: 'The acts of the sinful nature are obvious: sexual immorality, impurity . . . But the fruit of the Spirit is . . . self-control' (Galatians 5:19,22,23). 'No temptation has seized you except what is common to man. And God is faithful; he will not let you be tempted beyond what you can bear. But when you are tempted, he will also provide a way out so that you can stand up under it' (1 Corinthians 10:13).

We may want, but we do not need, a sexual partner. What we do need – and what God will provide for us, if we ask him – is one or two close friendships with those of our own sex. *Fresh Start* is a widely used American seminar in divorce recovery. It advises: 'Make clear in your mind the distinction between personal intimacy and physical, sexual (genital) intimacy. It is possible – indeed, it is very important – to learn to become an intimate person in ways that do not involve physical, sexual touch. For many people, the very word "intimacy" means physical sexual touching, but that is a very narrow use of the word. Intimacy means drawing close and being close to another . . . reveal[ing] my true self to you and trust[ing] you with that knowledge.'[31]

What if I find myself strongly attracted to another man/woman?

The teaching of the New Testament may be fine, but what if I find that I have fallen deeply in love with another man/woman? And he/she has fallen in love with me? Or what if we have gone further and got engaged before we began to understand the teaching of Christ about remarriage?

It cannot be stressed enough that there is grave danger, in the first few years after separation, in getting deeply involved in another relationship. Even those counsellors who see no reason not to marry at a later date almost always urge a gap of at least three years before beginning a new relationship: 'The promise of "love" is like a powerful narcotic. It relieves pain. It feels so good . . . But . . . a romantic relationship . . . can make us think we are healed when we are not, thereby causing us to ignore the true healing we need.'[32] Healing, as we have seen earlier, comes supremely through understanding what caused your marriage to break down, recognising your own faults in it and being able to talk and think about it calmly. That takes time.

But how about several years later, when a large measure of

healing has taken place? Chapman puts the truth very clearly: 'If you are not free to marry, you are not free to date.'[33] You are still married. That means not only that you are not free to remarry but that you are not at liberty to start a new romantic or sexual relationship. To do so would be unfair on yourself and unfair on the other person. If you have already begun a relationship and it has progressed a long way, you will need as gently but as clearly as possible to bring the relationship to an end, talking it through, asking forgiveness for the hurt you are causing but making it plain that you have no alternative but to end a relationship which, as you see it, cannot be God's will for you.

A new romantic involvement is not an option for the Christian divorcee. The *Fresh Start* seminar advises: 'Look for friends. Not just a special friend but a network of friends. You need love, compassion, support, helpfulness – with no possibility that anyone will take advantage of you. . . . People who love you without wanting anything in response (whereas in romantic relationships the other person certainly wants various things in response).[34]

Above all we are to relish and draw on the friendship of Christ himself. A young divorced woman said to me, 'I don't want to remarry, because of the freedom I have found [she was going to Bible College, she was working in a home for handicapped children and was involved in running a church youth group]. And because I have come to see that the Lord the creator is my husband, and if I married someone else, I'd have another husband. Of course God would still be my husband but I don't want to dilute that.' I asked her what would happen if she felt attracted to a man: 'I would break the bond before it got too far, just as one would do if attracted to a married man.' This is precisely what Paul is teaching in 1 Corinthians 7:32-35.

What about the strains of being a single parent?

The pressures on a single mum can be intense. Wouldn't it be better for her and for the whole family if she were to remarry?

In fact, remarriage is not the answer: mainly, of course, because Christ has made it clear that remarriage after divorce is adultery in God's eyes (see Chapter 7), but also because a new marriage frequently adds strains to the family rather than relieving them. Remarriage may make things easier or more difficult for the single parent (it will probably do both) but it will normally put further strains on the children and therefore on the whole family.

That is why many divorcees, even among those who allow the possibility of remarriage, put off developing a new relationship until after the children have grown up and left home. They know the children have suffered enough already without being at fault; many have felt the children should not have their home life further disrupted by the introduction of a step-parent.

But children do need good, healthy relationships with adults other than their mum. The most important factor for their psychological health and development is a relationship that is as close and regular as possible with their own father as well as their mother; this cannot be overstressed. Where this is simply not possible, it is very helpful for the boys, especially, to form a strong link with an adult (heterosexual) male. The custodial parent may need to ask for an already burgeoning friendship to be deliberately developed; many men are delighted by an invitation to become an honorary 'uncle', 'godfather' or 'grandfather'.

What if everybody around me has a completely different attitude to the single life from God's?

It would be so much easier if all our friends and family members knew about the New Testament's teaching on singleness and agreed with it. But the very opposite is the case. Most people have never thought about Christ's teaching on the single life or on singleness after divorce, and they have an abhorrence of permanent singleness. The result, very often, is that far from encouraging divorcees in their singleness, they are for ever introducing them to 'available' members of the opposite sex and seeking to matchmake. Christians are just as bad as others, if not worse. What can we do in the face of such pressure against remaining single?

You need quietly to explain what the New Testament says and then stick to your guns. I was struck by this recently in a different (though related) context. I met a young couple before their wedding and asked them whether or not they wanted to make the stronger promises in which the bride promises to 'obey' and the husband to 'serve' (I use this in preference to 'worship'). They asked me to explain what these added commitments meant in practice, and I sought, as far as possible, to be neutral in my explanation. I suggested they go away and think about it, and they told me later they had decided to make the strengthened promises.

They were not Christians and had no Christian background. When, at the rehearsal, we came to the vows, the best man made a great joke about the promise to obey. But the bride and groom were quite firm with him: 'We've thought about it. We've made our decision. We think it's right.'

You need to be equally clear and firm as you explain what you have discovered in the New Testament teaching about divorce and remarriage. You have decided to stay clear of any new relationship not just because God has said that remarriage is not open to you, but because the New Testament shows that the single life is good and in many ways even better than marriage (1 Corinthians 7:38).

It is that positive note which is the sign that you have truly assimilated – perhaps after a struggle of many months – the teaching of the New Testament. Jones can write of the ministry he is involved with: 'Perhaps the most encouraging aspect . . . is that, through the years, we have seen many single-again people truly celebrate their singleness. . . . They learned to be fulfilled and happy people, not . . . *in spite of* their singleness, but because they learned how to appreciate the opportunities of singleness and to make healthy choices about their lives.'[35]

Is it fair if I didn't want the divorce in the first place?

I can see that all this makes sense if I initiated the divorce; it doesn't seem right that I should be able to leave my husband (or wife) and then marry again as if nothing had happened. But what if I am the 'innocent party'? What if I never wanted this divorce and did everything possible to keep the marriage together? Is it fair then to forbid me remarriage?

No, the whole situation is not fair; but it is not God who has treated you unfairly. At your wedding, your husband (or wife) made you a very solemn promise: 'To have and to hold . . . to love and to cherish till death us do part.' He also said that he would 'be faithful to you as long as you both shall live'. He has gone back on his promise and, if you remained faithful to him, nothing can excuse that.

But you also made the same promise to him. You didn't promise that you would be faithful to him only while he remained faithful, that you would 'have and hold . . . love and cherish' him only if he kept his side of the bargain. On the contrary, you promised him this commitment of yourself 'for better for worse, for richer for poorer, in sickness and in health . . . till death us do part'. You have kept this promise and God is asking you to continue to keep it.

It will be so much easier for you if you don't kick against it. Being content with what God asks of us is not easy; it needs to be learned. But it is the only key to true happiness: 'I have learned to be content whatever the circumstances. I know what it is to be in need, and I know what it is to have plenty. I have learned the secret of being content in any and every situation . . . I can do everything through him who gives me strength' (Philippians 4:11-13). And then Paul adds, speaking specifically about financial need with which divorcees are often all too familiar: 'And my God will meet all your needs according to his glorious riches in Christ Jesus' (v. 19).

Does God really condemn me to singleness for the rest of my life?

This is how the question about singleness after divorce is often initially put. It is often how people feel. Yet I hope that if you have read this far you have begun to see that it is not an appropriate way to ask about the single life of the divorced man or woman.

In the first place, God cannot really be blamed for the pain and loneliness that you experience. God longs for you and your partner to be back together. His great desire is for you to come to the point where you can forgive each other, establish new patterns of relating to each other and be reconciled. When he says that if there is a divorce you 'must remain unmarried or else be reconciled' to your partner (1 Corinthians 7:11), there is no doubt which option he would prefer.

If this is impossible, either for the time being or for ever, it is not God who has placed you in this position. You and your partner knew what you were giving yourselves to when you got married. You were committing yourselves to each other 'for the whole of your earthly life'.

But in the second place, and far more importantly, singleness is not a sentence. It is not a life to which you have been 'condemned'. Of course it has some very painful disadvantages, especially if it has come about because of the breakup of a once-cherished marriage. But the Bible points us to a very real counterbalance, to some positive and precious advantages of being single again, if only we will gradually learn to accept them.

Certainly it will take time to learn how to use our singleness to 'please the Lord' rather than any other human being, to grow in holiness 'in body and spirit' and to 'live . . . in undivided devotion to the Lord' (1 Corinthians 7:32-35). But if we let God himself give us this new perspective on the single life and take the opportunity to grow spiritually through our singleness, we will be able to see that it can be not a 'sentence of condemnation' but a 'gift' (1 Corinthians 7:7; Matthew 19:11).

Joseph was abominably treated by his brothers who should have protected him. He suffered a great deal because of them. But later on he was able to look back and say, 'As for you, you meant evil against me; but God meant it for good' (Genesis 50:20, RSV). It often takes time to get to the point where we can genuinely say that, but if we ask God to work in us and change us, we will be able from our experience to say the same.

God will not fail us throughout our lives. He has promised: 'Listen to me, O house of Jacob . . . you whom I have . . . carried since your birth. Even to your old age and grey hairs I am he, I am he who will sustain you. I have made you and I will carry you; I will sustain you and I will rescue you' (Isaiah 46:3,4). And God doesn't break his promise.

How can my experience bring hope and encouragement to others?

When our marriage first breaks up, we tend to turn in on ourselves: to nurse our pain, to be very conscious of our unfulfilled needs. It is understandable that, while we do so, we will probably see the separation, and later the divorce, in an almost wholly negative light.

Gradually, healing comes. We still have days of terrible bleakness, but as the months, and then the first few years, pass we begin to be able to look away from ourselves and look out to the needs of others. Then we find something extraordinary and wonderful: that God can use our pain – or rather, the way he has met with us in our pain and the hope he has given us – to help others.

At one point in his life Paul had been 'under great pressure, far beyond [his] ability to endure' (2 Corinthians 1:8). We don't know whether this was from some very severe, almost fatal, illness (he 'despaired even of life', [v. 8]) or whether it was because of intense persecution from his enemies who were certainly very active at this time. What we do know is that in his suffering he found God to be 'the Father of compassion and the God of all comfort, who comforts us in all our troubles' (vv. 3,4).

But he also saw very clearly that this new closeness to God was not something to be kept to himself. Rather, it had been given to him by God 'so that we can comfort those in any trouble with the comfort we ourselves have received from God' (v. 4).

Divorcees, who have known not only pain but God's meeting them in their pain, can often be the channels of God's help to others in pain. They may not have suffered in precisely the same way, but the person who most helps someone struggling with the agony of separation is often himself (or herself) a divorcee. One woman had been in deep depression for many months after her husband left her. Many people helped her gradually to recover, but there was a definite turning-point: 'June [someone who had been divorced earlier and had also known bitter depression] . . . was instrumental in my climb back to God. . . . In the space of an hour she turned my inner despair and desperation to hope.'

Margaret Evening tells of a decisive moment when she saw how her singleness could be used to help others. She was reading Elizabeth Goudge's novel *The Dean's Watch* in which a physically disabled woman gradually realises that a career and marriage are not likely to be possible for her. Margaret Evening came to this passage in the novel: 'With no prospects of a career or marriage, it seemed that she was doomed to lifelong boredom. But then in a moment of awakening, it dawned upon her that *loving* could be a vocation in itself, a life work. It could be a career, like marriage, or nursing, or going on stage. . . . Quietly she accepted the vocation and took a vow to love.' Reading this was for Evening 'a sudden moment of clarity . . . I knew that God was placing upon me a vocation for life'. She began immediately by inviting a lonely person round for the weekend.[36]

Key verses

'The Lord gave, and the Lord has taken away; blessed be the name of the Lord' (Job 1:21, RSV).
'I love you, O Lord, my strength' (Psalm 18:1).

CHAPTER 9

QUESTIONS ABOUT GOD'S FORGIVENESS

Becky realised within weeks of marrying Jason that she'd made a mistake. She saw increasingly that they had so little in common. Certainly he had no real interest in her Christian faith. And anyway they spent less and less time together. Each month he seemed to spend more evenings out with his friends, playing snooker or drinking. When he was at home, he just sat in front of the TV and expected to be waited on; or he came in late, reeking of drink, finding fault with anything she did and wanting only one thing from her: easy sex. But she found it was becoming abhorrent to her, to be pawed by this lout of a husband.

She stuck it out for five years, though many of her friends were urging her to leave him. Then one night he bawled obscenities at her about her parents and she could bear it no longer. She packed a suitcase and left.

Most people told her she had done the right thing, including some of her Christian friends. Her pastor was generous, understanding and non-committal. She prayed long and hard about what had happened, talked to others for many hours and felt she had done the right thing. Certainly it was a great relief to be away from Jason. But then, three months later, she was suddenly overcome by remorse. She tried to make it up with

Jason but he had already started a relationship with another woman. She felt that she had gone against all that Christ taught about marriage, all that she had promised in her vows. She stopped going to church, because she felt so guilty. Could God possibly forgive?

If God 'hates divorce', does he hate me because I'm divorced?

The Bible puts it so clearly: '"I hate divorce," says the Lord God of Israel' (Malachi 2:16). Since he says categorically that he hates divorce, doesn't it follow that he must hate me because I'm divorced?

It doesn't. But you are right to face up to Malachi 2. We must first understand, and give due weight to, God's very definite statement: 'I hate divorce.' Then we can also see clearly his true attitude to you as a divorcee.

A few verses earlier in Malachi 2, God says that he 'is acting as the witness between you and the wife of your youth, . . . the wife of your marriage covenant' (v. 14). It seems there were always, or often, designated witnesses to a marriage agreement in Old Testament times (Ruth 4:9-13), and Malachi says that when any 'marriage covenant' is made, God is the principal 'witness between you and the wife of your youth'.

At weddings in our own day, witnesses sign the marriage register. They are often the couple's parents or close friends. But, whether you married in church or before a registrar or judge, it is God who was the principal witness, present at your wedding. He confirmed your marriage then; he seeks to protect it now.

The Bible picture goes further than that. God was not only the main witness at your wedding. He is the parent who gave you to each other. In the story of Genesis 2, from which Christ and the New Testament writers draw their main teaching about marriage, 'the Lord God . . . brought her [the woman] to the man' (v. 22). 'God himself, like a father of the bride, leads the woman to the man.'[37]

It is because he is both the principal witness of the original marriage and the father who gave the bride away that divorce grieves him so deeply. This is why Jesus said, 'What God has joined together, let man not separate' (Mark 10:9; Matthew 19:6). It is why God himself says, 'I hate divorce' (Malachi 2:16).

But that is not at all to say that he hates you. Isaiah depicts a time when the Israelites felt that God had turned his back on them: 'Zion said, "The Lord has forsaken me, the Lord has forgotten me."' But God replies, 'Can a mother forget the baby at her breast and have no compassion on the child she has borne? Though she may forget, I will not forget you! See, I have engraved you on the palms of my hands' (Isaiah 49:14-16).

This is an instructive passage because it acknowledges that some of those with the closest ties to us can desert us. Isaiah says that mothers sometimes desert their own children; we know from experience that wives can desert their husbands, and husbands can desert their wives. It is a natural reaction in those situations to think that God has deserted us too (see v. 14), not only because he has let it happen but because we feel worthless and guilty. But God says he is quite unlike the partner who has left us: 'I will not forget you! See, I have engraved you on the palms of my hands' (vv. 15,16).

Even if you took the initiative in divorcing your partner, and even if you can see now that you should not have done so, God hates the divorce certainly but that doesn't mean that he hates you.

The Israelites had sinned badly down the centuries: they were 'arrogant and stiff-necked'. But in Nehemiah's day the Israelite leaders confessed this sin and were able to say, 'You are a forgiving God, gracious and compassionate, slow to anger and abounding in love. Therefore you did not desert them' (Nehemiah 9:16,17).

All that is asked of us is to repent of any sins that we may have contributed to the breakup of the marriage and to determine to follow God's instructions with his help. Then, far from his hating us, we can be assured that he loves us and forgives us and sticks by us.

Is God saying that divorce is the unforgivable sin?

Many Christians think that Christ's teaching on remarriage means that divorce must be an unforgivable sin. After all, they reason, if a divorcee must not remarry, if a remarriage is in fact adultery (Matthew 5:32; Mark 10:11,12; Matthew 19:9; Luke 16:18), then this must mean that God has been unable to forgive the divorce. If he could really forgive the divorce, he would allow divorcees to remarry.

This is a very widely held view. It is normally met in the form: 'If the Church forbids remarriage, then the Church must think divorce is an unforgivable sin.' People say that this is the Church's teaching because it is comparatively easy to dismiss the teaching of the Church and they don't want to acknowledge, and face up to, the teaching of Christ on remarriage.

But the view that divorce is an unforgivable sin is based on a fundamental misunderstanding. It is not because of the divorce that a divorcee is forbidden to remarry; it is because of the original marriage. Christ does not say that I must refrain from remarriage because I am divorced but because I am still married. That is why, in answer to a question on divorce, Christ goes back to marriage and explains that in marriage a couple 'become one flesh' and are 'joined together by God'. It is why he calls remarriage 'adultery' (Mark 10:2-12; Matthew 19:3-9).

Of course there is sin in the breakup of a marriage, and normally there is at least some measure of sin on both sides. But that sin, whatever it is and however extensive, can be fully forgiven. One of the greatest sins a married partner can commit is adultery. This must be so because adultery makes divorce, which God hates, permissible (Matthew 5:32; 19:9). Yet even adultery can be fully forgiven. Paul can say, 'Do you not know that the wicked will not inherit the kingdom of God? Do not be deceived: Neither the sexually immoral . . . nor adulterers nor male prostitutes nor homosexual offenders . . . will inherit the kingdom of God. And that is what some of you were. But you

were washed, you were sanctified, you were justified in the name
of the Lord Jesus Christ and by the Spirit of our God' (1
Corinthians 6:9-11).

Of course we need to repent. Of course we need to confess
and forsake any sins we have committed against God and our
marriage partner (1 John 1:8-10). But when we repent, God
'washes . . . sanctifies . . . justifies' us (1 Corinthians 6:11).
There is nothing in marriage breakup and divorce that cannot
and will not be fully forgiven.

If God fully forgives my divorce, doesn't that leave me free to remarry?

But then if that is the case, why may I not remarry? If God really
has forgiven me and washed the slate entirely clean, surely
remarriage becomes a possibility for me?

No. Two things have happened. You have got married; and
you have been divorced. In the eyes of the law, you got married
and are no longer married, because you are legally divorced. But
in the eyes of God you got married and are still married, despite
your legal, and perhaps morally legitimate, divorce.

The proof of this is that remarriage on your part would be, as
Christ teaches, adultery. Remarriage is adultery not because you
are divorced but because you are still married. God can and does
forgive any repentant person's marital sin – he forgives any sins
you may have committed within the marriage or at the time of
your divorce or since the divorce – but that forgiveness does not
undo your marriage. Forgiveness sets us free from sin and guilt,
not from being married.

Isn't God the God of second chances?

But when we sin and repent, surely God doesn't leave us where
we are? Isn't one of the great features of the Christian God
that he doesn't write anybody off, that he is always willing to

give us a second (and third, and hundredth) chance?

Yes. The greatest way in which he shows himself to be the God of new beginnings is in his gift of forgiveness: 'Who is a God like you who pardons sin and forgives . . . the transgression? . . . You will again have compassion on us; you will tread our sins underfoot and hurl all our iniquities into the depths of the sea' (Micah 7:18,19). We may feel a continuing sense of guilt, but our guilt is no longer there in God's eyes. It has been buried in the depths of the sea. If Christ tells Simon Peter to forgive innumerable times (Matthew 18:21,22), he himself will surely forgive still more often.

Forgiveness and returning to a right relationship with God are offered to all. In addition, God offers the divorcee two options for a second chance, a new life. These are clearly spelled out in 1 Corinthians 7:11 – 'If she does [divorce], she must remain unmarried or else be reconciled to her husband.'

Both options are, or can be, signs of God's grace. Reconciliation is his great desire: not the re-establishment of past, destructive patterns of life together, but the gradual development of new, healthy patterns within which the marriage relationship can be healed and begin to grow.

If this is not possible, singleness is what God gives (compare 1 Corinthians 7:7). This is an opportunity for a fresh start, a new life of growing closeness to Christ and devotion to Christ (1 Corinthians 7:32-35). This 'undivided' affection for Christ will bring gradual healing for the past as well as personal growth in the present.

The only option that God does not offer us is a second marriage. He cannot. In his eyes we are still married.

If a Christian gets married, quickly realises he has made a mistake and then falls in love with another woman, we cannot say that God is the God of second chances and will therefore allow him to divorce his wife, just because he is no longer in love with her, and marry the woman he has fallen for. This option is not open to him because he is married. It is for precisely the same reason that a divorcee may not remarry. In God's eyes and therefore in fact, he is still married; he is not free to take a second wife.

What if I don't feel fully forgiven?

It is hard to feel forgiven as a divorcee. It is common to veer between feelings of anger and guilt, whether we have initiated the separation or been deserted. We feel we've let so many people down: our marriage partner whom we can't have satisfied, our children who've been robbed of life with both parents, our family who are heartbroken, our friends who no longer know what to say to us, and our God whom we have grieved. That is how it can seem; and with such a weight of guilt feelings, it's hard to believe we are fully forgiven.

It will be a continuing, though gradually less intense, struggle. One fundamental issue is this: Whom are you going to trust, your feelings or your God? God is described in this way: 'The Lord is compassionate and gracious, slow to anger, abounding in love . . . He does not treat us as our sins deserve or repay us according to our iniquities. For as high as the heavens are above the earth, so great is his love for those who fear him; as far as the east is from the west, so far has he removed our transgressions from us' (Psalm 103:8-12). That is how God has revealed himself. It is the truth and needs to be clung to, despite our self-accusing feelings.

Hezekiah expresses this graphically. He says of God: 'You have put all my sins behind your back' (Isaiah 38:17). Having put them there out of sight, God has no intention of turning round and looking at them again. We need not either.

What if only a successful second marriage would make me feel fully forgiven?

Almost all divorcees wrestle with feelings of guilt; many find it hard to feel entirely forgiven, and some imagine that a second marriage will be the answer that will lay the ghost of guilt to rest. Actually a second marriage is very unlikely to rid us of our sense of guilt. In fact if that is part of your hopes for a second marriage, you will carry your feelings of guilt into that new marriage, and they may well cripple the very marriage you had pinned such hopes on. To marry or even to start going out with someone in order to heal hurts in our life is a very unstable foundation for a new relationship.

Instead, we have to learn, painfully slow though this may be, to rely on the facts and not on our feelings. The fact is that we are fully forgiven, if we have confessed and repented of past sins; God has repeatedly promised his forgiveness. The fact is that Christ has said to remarry is to commit adultery; if therefore I go ahead and enter a second marriage in the hope that I will feel fully forgiven, I am actually committing another act of disobedience. The fact is that remarriage will not free me from guilt but add a further sin for which I will need further forgiveness.

Feeling forgiven is not at all easy; but a second marriage is not the answer.

How can I learn to forgive myself?

This is a very important question. It may be hard to accept that God really has forgiven me; it is often harder still to forgive myself.

The first step must be a decisive facing up to our own faults, to the sins, the misjudgements and the selfishness that we contributed to our marriage. Paradoxically those who find it hardest to forgive themselves can also (sometimes, not always) be those who believe that ninety per cent of the fault was their partner's. But the road to finding peace within ourselves normally begins by acknowledging the considerable amount that we contributed to the pain of the marriage.

Ask God to show you the faults that you brought to the

marriage, the sins that you committed. 'All a man's ways seem right to him, but the Lord weighs the heart' (Proverbs 21:2). 'All a man's ways seem innocent to him, but motives are weighed by the Lord' (Proverbs 16:2, compare Luke 16:15). The purpose of this is not of course to wallow in your sinfulness but to have as full and realistic a picture as possible of what needs to be confessed to God and then forgiven by him.

Many have found it helpful to write the list down. This helps to order and clarify our thoughts. Then you need to go through the list again, specifically confessing each fault and asking God to forgive it.

You know that God forgives every sin that you confess, but it can be an enormous help to have this demonstrated in some way. Several have found it helpful to burn the list that they have made, as a symbol that their guilt has been removed (compare the symbolism of the live coal in Isaiah 6:5-7). Others have been offered, or asked for, a simple communion service. One man wrote how this was an important turning point for him. He went into church with his minister and about eight close friends. He himself confessed his sin (in general terms, though he had prepared specifically for this time) and each friend read a relevant passage from the Bible or said a prayer. 'Conrad [the minister] prayed that now I would be able to put the past behind me and that I should feel accepted without any more fear . . . It was the most uplifting experience I have ever had in my entire life.'

The joy of knowing that we have been forgiven is exhilarating and draws out our love for Jesus. A woman of the streets knew that she had gone deep into sexual sin. In fact, it was common knowledge. Others were ashamed to be anywhere near her. She was initially ashamed in front of Jesus. But she was also drawn to him; she knew that he could bring her the forgiveness she longed for. The proof that she knew 'her many sins [had] been forgiven' was that she showed such deep love in weeping over Jesus, and kissing his feet, and pouring costly perfume on them (Luke 7:36-50).

Of course feelings of guilt will reappear from time to time. Ken Crispin says that we will need to train ourselves to respond immediately: 'Well, thank God I'm forgiven and I don't have to feel guilty any more.'[38]

How can I learn to forgive my partner?

Forgiveness of our partner is not an option for us; it is an obligation, even though it may prove to be one of the hardest things God asks of us. To withhold forgiveness is to hurt God; to learn forgiveness is to imitate God: 'Do not grieve the Holy Spirit of God, with whom you were sealed for the day of redemption. Get rid of all bitterness, rage and anger, brawling and slander, along with every form of malice. Be kind and compassionate to one another, forgiving each other, just as in Christ God forgave you' (Ephesians 4:30-32).

Of course that is a great deal easier said than done. It may be best to begin by realising how much harm bitterness does to you. 'If I go back and back over the old hurts and my grudges, it doesn't hurt the person who has hurt me; it only screws me up still more.'[39] Jones says that we need to apply specifically to our anger and bitterness the general Christian principle found in Philippians 3:13,14 – 'Forgetting what is behind and straining towards what is ahead, I press on towards the goal to win the prize for which God has called me heavenwards in Christ Jesus.'

Then it can be enormously helpful to write a letter to your partner, even if you never send it or have no intention of sending it. As you think what to write and then begin writing, there are three things which you might ask from God.

One is for the perspective of God himself. Joyce Huggett writes: 'Ask God to show you how he feels about your partner,' and adds: 'Wait for an answer to your question!'[40]

Secondly, you can ask God to help you to be fair to your partner. Chapman suggests that you begin to examine yourself, using Christ's words: 'Why do you look at the speck of sawdust in your brother's eye and pay no attention to the plank in your own eye? . . . First take the plank out of your own eye, and then you will see clearly to remove the speck from your brother's eye' (Matthew 7:3-5). 'In a quiet setting, with time to reflect, say to God: "Lord, where have I failed my [partner]? You and I both know how that person has failed me, but right now I want to concentrate on my own failures". List . . . whatever comes to mind. Be as specific as you can. Include failures when you were living together and failures since you have been separated.'[41]

Thirdly, you can ask God to help you understand your partner. It was this that seems to have helped Jesus to forgive those who were so hostile to him: 'Father forgive them, for they do not know what they are doing' (Luke 23:34). If you can see the marriage from the point of view of your partner, with his or her hopes and dashed expectations, and if you can see that he or she often acted out of ignorance or even good motives, it will go a long way towards enabling you to forgive.

But there is a further stage still for the Christian. Of course we need to understand our partner's circumstances and why he acted as he did; this will at least in part excuse him. But this, says C. S. Lewis, 'is not Christian charity; it is only fair-mindedness. To be a Christian means to forgive the inexcusable, because God has forgiven the inexcusable in you.'[42]

Of course forgiveness is a long-term process. Those who say after a week or a month, 'I've forgiven her,' have hardly even begun. There are levels of forgiveness, and we will find that with God's help we are able to forgive more deeply and thoroughly as the years go by.

But we've got to want to forgive: 'True forgiveness involves not warm feelings but the will . . . The question to ask yourself is not "can I forgive?" but "will I forgive?"'[43] So we need to be determined not to nurse our grievances and tell them to others, but to learn gradually to forgive. Our forgiveness of our partner mirrors God's forgiveness of us.

Key verses

'You have put all my sins behind your back' (Isaiah 38:17).
'As far as the east is from the west, so far has he removed our transgressions from us' (Psalm 103:12).
'Be kind and compassionate to one another, forgiving each other, just as in Christ God forgave you' (Ephesians 4:32).

CHAPTER 10

QUESTIONS ABOUT RECONCILIATION

Mike felt torn apart. He was very angry with Susan for leaving him and for all the accusations of caring only for himself which she hurled at him; but he also still loved her, despite it all. He wanted to break off all ties with her, have nothing to do with her; but he was also desperate to know what she was doing and whom she was seeing.

Mike was a Christian. He see-sawed with his own conflicting feelings, but he wanted to know what God was asking of him. They were separated, but should he accept that? Should he now have as little to do with Susan as possible? Or was it right to hope that they might get back together again?

How much should I keep in touch with my partner?

We return to 1 Corinthians 7:11. Here Paul, as part of his quotation of Christ's teaching, says that two options are open to the divorcee: 'If she does [divorce], she must remain unmarried or else be reconciled to her husband.' There is no doubt which option God himself prefers: 'The entire Bible is a record of God's attempts to be reconciled to his people.'⁴⁴

You may not be ready yet for any active steps towards recon-

154

ciliation; your partner may not be ready. But if you lose touch with your partner, you effectively rule out God's preferred option of reconciliation; whereas if you keep in touch with your partner, you remain open to the possibility of being reconciled.

If you have children, there is a further reason for keeping in touch. They need regular, consistent time spent with both of their parents under agreed arrangements that are as free from strain as possible. To achieve this aim, you and your partner will need to stay in regular contact and to keep your relationship as amicable as you can. If you were to fulfil all your children's desires, you would work at renewing your marriage, since that is almost certainly what would give them greatest pleasure.

But children are not the only reason for staying in touch. Even if you have no children, God's call is very clearly expressed: 'Do not repay anyone evil for evil . . . If it is possible, as far as it depends on you, live at peace with everyone' (Romans 12:17,18). This is God's will in all relationships; how much more in the relationship between marriage partners.

Why should I even want reconciliation?

My head can tell me that I ought to 'live at peace with' my partner, but my heart rebels against it, after all the wrong she's done me. Why should I want to work for reconciliation?

Because of Christ. He lived and died to bring reconciliation between parties that had fallen out: reconciliation between humans and God, and also reconciliation between human and human.

Ephesians 2 describes what was one of the greatest problems for the early Church: the mutual suspicion of Jews and Gentiles. There was a 'dividing wall' between them; there was bitter 'hostility'. But Christ died to break down these barriers: 'He himself is our peace, who has made the two one and has destroyed the barrier, the dividing wall of hostility . . . His purpose was to create in himself one new man out of the two, thus making peace, and in this one body to reconcile both of them to God through the cross, by which he put to death their hostility [towards one another]. He came and preached peace to you who were far away and peace to those who were near' (vv. 14-17).

Christ's whole work was to bring reconciliation. It is described here in two ways: where there has been 'hostility' (vv. 14,16), he wants to 'be our peace', to 'make peace', to 'preach peace' (vv 14,15,17); and where there has been a 'dividing wall' (v. 14), he 'makes the two one', he 'creates . . . one new man out of the two' (vv. 14,15). This last expression has echoes of Christ's teaching about marriage: 'The two become one flesh. So they are no longer two, but one' (Mark 10:8; Matthew 19:5,6).

In harbouring bitterness and hostility, therefore, we side with Christ's enemies and destroy all that Christ died for. In working for peace and reconciliation, we prove ourselves Christ's friends and build on the achievements of his death. It is for Christ's sake, and for love of his cross, that we walk the difficult path of working towards reconciliation with our marriage partner.

Is reconciliation possible when I'm so angry?

Your anger is very understandable. Your partner also is almost certainly angry and hurt. It is true that anger makes reconciliation considerably more difficult, and if your partner has just said something, or done something, which has made your anger flare up again, this is not the moment to be in contact with him or to suggest you talk. 'Speak when you are angry,' says Ambrose Bierce, 'and you will make the best speech you will ever regret.'

Nevertheless, you cannot wait until you have no trace of anger left before you start working for reconciliation. In the Sermon on the Mount, Jesus warns about the consequences of anger: 'I tell you that anyone who is angry with his brother will be subject to judgment. Again, anyone who says to his brother, "Raca," [a term of contempt] is answerable to the Sanhedrin. But anyone who says, "You fool!" will be in danger of the fire of hell.' He then immediately explains how to deal with anger, and his solution is actively to seek reconciliation: 'Therefore, if you are offering your gift at the altar and there remember that your brother has something against you, leave your gift there in front of the altar. First go and be reconciled to your brother' (Matthew 5:22-24). It is significant that the scenario starts with our anger (v. 22) and begins to be resolved when we realise that the person we are angry with 'has something against us' (v. 23). In other words, anger subsides as we recognise that we too have frequently sinned in the relationship, as well as having been sinned against.

Anger also subsides as we pray. Jesus teaches in the same chapter: 'You have heard that it was said, "Love your neighbour and hate your enemy." But I tell you: Love your enemies and pray for those who persecute you, that you may be sons of your Father in heaven' (vv. 43-45). It is possible to pray prayers that are just veiled criticisms of your partner and further accusations. But if you pray for his or her welfare, it will be an important step on the way to reconciliation and a way of gradually conquering your anger.

Is reconciliation possible with someone from whom I'm divorced?

Certainly. The classic example here is the prophet Hosea. According to the traditional and most likely interpretation of his autobiographical material, he married a woman named Gomer (1:2,3). She had an affair (she may have been or become a prostitute) and committed adultery (3:1). Hosea and she certainly separated, and very probably divorced since he had to buy her back from another to whom she belonged (3:2). Yet in this situation, when he could be forgiven for washing his hands of her completely, 'The Lord said to me, "Go show your love to your wife again, though she is loved by another and is an adulteress. Love her as the Lord loves the Israelites"' (3:1).

That last sentence shows how Hosea's love, and our love in working for reconciliation with a partner who has wronged us deeply, mirrors the love of God. Throughout the book of Hosea, God is pictured as the husband against whom his wife Israel has committed constant adultery. Probably he has divorced her (her phrase 'my former husband', the most likely translation of 2:7, implies this; compare Jeremiah 3:8). Yet God is determined to seek reconciliation, to woo her back (2:14-23).

Of course divorce makes reconciliation more difficult. It may seem to you impossible now; any remaining hope has gone. But your partner's feelings are probably much more variable than he or she likes to admit. She may sound determined and firm and yet sometimes be very uncertain about whether she has done the right thing.

Anyway circumstances change, especially when a new relationship doesn't work out: 'She will chase after her lovers but not catch them; she will look for them but not find them. Then she will say, "I will go back to my husband as at first [or rather: "my former husband"], for then I was better off than now"' (Hosea 2:7).

A couple whom I know well divorced. She had an affair with a man she played table tennis with and had a child by him. Her divorced husband in reaction also had an affair which almost wrecked their chances of reconciliation. Yet they continued to see each other because they were determined that the children should have full, almost unrestricted, access to both. And when both affairs petered out, happily at the same time, they came to realise that they had given up a basically good, if skewed, relationship too easily. They worked to establish a new relationship, married again in a registry office (they were never unmarried as far as Christ is concerned) and are happily married today.

Chapman rightly comments that a great deal depends on our attitude in working for reconciliation: 'Don't say "I might fail", but rather "I might succeed."'[45] That is certainly God's desire.

What if my partner doesn't want anything to do with reconciliation?

Of course it needs two to work at reconciliation. If your partner does not want to be involved, you will not be able to achieve reconciliation now. You should not pester him; it will only be counterproductive. Paul states this principle in relation to contesting a separation: 'If the unbeliever leaves, let him do so. A believing man or woman is not bound [literally: 'enslaved'] in such circumstances; God has called us to live in peace' (1 Corinthians 7:15). In other words, you will only stir up further hostility if you fight tooth and nail against a separation that the other partner has determined on.

Much the same principle applies over our seeking reconciliation. If we continually badger a reluctant partner, we will make the situation more difficult and ultimate reconciliation less likely. I have known situations in which a separated Christian has refused to take 'no' for an answer and has only made an already strained relationship much worse. But, as we have seen already, the answer may not be 'no' for ever. Too many people try once to achieve reconciliation and, when that fails, give up.

Far better is to seek, hard though it is, to imitate God: 'God demonstrates his own love for us in this: while we were yet sinners, Christ died for us . . . When we were God's enemies, we were reconciled to him through the death of his Son' (Romans 5:8,10). 'Once you were alienated from God and were enemies in your minds because of your evil behaviour. But now he has reconciled you' (Colossians 1:21,22). God was committed to reconciliation even while we were hostile to him; we must be committed to reconciliation with our partner, even if he or she is at the moment hostile to us. Christ was prepared to wait until we turned from our hostility and were open to him; we must be prepared to wait for our partner.

You may think: '"It sounds good, but it won't work. We've

tried before. Besides, I don't think my spouse will even try again." Perhaps you are right, but do not assume that the hostile attitude of your spouse will remain for ever . . . Two months [or two years] from now . . . your mate may be willing to talk.'[46]

Chapman has a splendid passage on 'Love is patient, love is kind' (1 Corinthians 13:4). On love's patience, he says, 'Don't get in a hurry. Your marriage did not fall apart overnight and it will not be rebuilt today.' Be patient with quite contradictory remarks from your partner. He is not lying. He is expressing the conflicting emotions and thoughts within him: one moment wanting to get back together, the next repelled by all the hurt, the next attracted to another woman. It is even more helpful if you can say: "I understand that you are pulled in two directions. I feel that myself."[47]

On love's kindness, Chapman says that before and during separation we often speak destructive words to and about our partner, but 'reconciliation is paved with words of kindness'. Your partner, like you, is feeling bad about all that has happened; find kind words that will build him up – for example, the occasional (not too frequent) phone call to find out how he is doing to show that you care. Kind actions – such as doing DIY jobs for a separated partner – go a long way too; and they begin to open up the possibility of reconciliation.[48]

Is it right or healthy to go on hoping?

Isn't it better to acknowledge that the marriage is over, to give up any hope of reconciliation and to build a new life? Some whose partners have left them seek deliberately to kill off any remnants of love they feel in order to get over the hurts and disappointments faster. Several people have said to me, 'I am deliberately trying to make myself bitter.' Even if this is not a wise approach, is it really healthy to go on hoping?

I think it is important to distinguish between an active seeking for reconciliation and a passive openness to it. Initially it is important actively to seek for reconciliation, not to accept too quickly that this separation will last, that divorce is inevitable. If, however, your partner steadfastly rejects any suggestion of trying to work on the relationship, this needs to be accepted emotionally. Those who refuse to believe or accept that they are going to be separated for some time, and perhaps for ever, prolong their own pain.

Yet that does not mean that we in turn harden ourselves against future reconciliation. On the contrary, we need to remain constantly open to reconciliation and ready to move – if hopeful signs appear – into active seeking for reconciliation again. We must beware of thinking, 'He/she'll never change.' He/she will change, and so will you. It may well be (although of course there is no guarantee of this) that these changes will make a new, better relationship possible.

What does it mean to 'seek actively for reconciliation'? It means wanting to be different ourselves, concentrating on changes we need to make rather than those our partner must make; it means acknowledging the faults we contributed to the marriage and asking our partner's forgiveness; it means gently sharing our desire to start a new and better relationship; it means not pressurising him or her, giving them time to decide whether they want to try a new way forward. I expand on all this in the last question of this chapter.

What does it mean to 'be passively open to reconciliation'? It means keeping in touch with your partner as frequently as you can bear and he or she will allow. It means keeping free from any other romantic or sexual relationship: 'Part of the [high] price [of reconciliation] is your personal freedom. You may see what you consider the opportunity of a lifetime slip away in terms of a new relationship.'[49] It means being available for reconciliation not just for a few weeks or months, but for life.

As a Christian, you need both to accept and not accept your divorce. If your partner is not (at least for the foreseeable future) open to reconciliation, it is vital that you accept this fact and start to build new, healthy patterns of life. But it is also important that you do not accept the divorce as final, and so remain open to reconciliation whenever the opportunity may come.

Isn't it better to cut myself off completely?

It is very understandable that you should want to cut yourself off completely from your partner. You hope it may staunch the pain. Yet this is an absolutely disastrous policy if there are children involved. It often happens that the father cuts himself off from his family either immediately or gradually over the months. We have seen in Chapter 5 that this is very detrimental to children's happiness and psychological growth.

It is also contrary to the will of God. John the Baptist was sent to prepare the way for Christ. This is how God described his task: 'He will go on before the Lord, in the spirit and power of Elijah, to turn the hearts of the fathers to their children' (Luke 1:17; compare Malachi 4:6 where he is also said to 'turn . . . the hearts of the children to their fathers'). It must therefore be God's will to establish and strengthen the relationship of fathers and children; and it is almost impossible to accomplish this if the father doesn't have a reasonably good relationship with the mother.

But even when there are no children involved, we are called to 'make every effort to live in peace with all men and to be holy' (Hebrews 12:14). Significantly the next verse goes on to speak of the need to root out any bitterness: 'See to it that no-one misses the grace of God and that no bitter root grows up to cause trouble and defile many' (v. 15). And the following verse reminds us to remain pure sexually: 'See that no-one is sexually immoral' (v. 16; compare 13:4). Bitterness and sexual sin are strong temptations for the divorced, but the fight against both is made considerably easier if we are working towards reconciliation with our husband or wife.

Cutting yourself off entirely from your partner avoids the problems, or tries to. It doesn't deal with them. There are of course some situations – for example, where there is continuing physical abuse – where a total withdrawal is necessary. But in the large majority of cases, it is far better, though initially more painful, to keep in touch with your partner and seek increasingly to 'live in peace'.

Is reconciliation still required if my partner has remarried?

Obviously full reconciliation is impossible if your partner has remarried. It would only be adding evil to evil if you tried to break up the second marriage. But that doesn't mean that you can now wash your hands of your partner. 'Make every effort to live in peace with all men' (Hebrews 12:14) certainly includes seeking to be at peace with the man or woman you married.

People often assume that reconciliation between marriage partners can only mean their living together permanently again with their marriage fully restored. This is certainly the ultimate goal, wherever it is possible. But reconciliation is broader than that. Talley defines it in this way: 'Reconciliation has been accomplished when both of you can carry on normal human communication,' that is: without bitterness, knots in your stomach or your voice rising.[50] That may be extremely hard to achieve but it is part of 'making efforts to live in peace with' the person you married.

And with his or her new partner. This can be harder still but is particularly important when you have children. If you are at loggerheads with your husband's (or wife's) new partner, it is your children who will suffer, because their vital contact with their other parent will be soured or even come to an end. If you can find the strength to be civil with the new partner, and to have, as far as possible, 'normal human communication' with her or him, it is your children who will gain, through happier time spent with their other parent.

It is not easy to love the person who has won the affection of the person you married and has usurped your place. But God's great desire – and therefore our goal – is for us to live at peace with our fellow humans, especially those who are close to us and our children.

Can I be healed fully if I have to keep thinking about my failed marriage?

For a time after my separation, I did nothing but think about what had happened. It was a very painful time. Now I am trying to forget. All this talk of learning to forgive my partner and working for reconciliation with him, or being open to reconciliation, merely stirs up muddy waters. Can I really be healed from all the pain if I keep on thinking about our marriage?

That depends on your thoughts. If, every time you think of your marriage, you sense the bitterness and anger rising again, if every thought of your partner merely fuels further resentment, then continuing to think about your marriage won't bring healing. But to suppress those thoughts, and to refuse to face them and begin to deal with them, is not the way of healing either. If we pretend we have 'come to terms with' our divorce and there is still seething bitterness within, we are deceiving ourselves and making it harder for God to heal us: 'Anyone who claims to be in the light but hates his brother is still in the darkness' (1 John 2:9).

Rather, healing begins when we face up to our inner anger. Of course, rooting out the bitterness and being healed of the consuming anger takes time. But if, over a period of time, there can be a real measure of reconciliation – sincere forgiveness, even some renewed friendship – then genuine healing will have taken place.

Meanwhile, we do have some choice over how we direct our thoughts. As you think of your partner and your marriage, try to turn your mind to those things that were good and for which you can be grateful: 'Whatever is true, whatever is noble, whatever is right, whatever is pure, whatever is lovely, whatever is admirable – if anything is excellent or praiseworthy – think about such things . . . And the God of peace will be with you' (Philippians 4:8,9).

How can I make the first moves towards reconciliation?

The first essential is to *keep yourself free from any new relationship*. If you are already involved in a new relationship, you will need as gently but as decisively as possible to break it off. Very often one partner leaves and the other, partly in revenge, seeks a new sexual or romantic relationship. When the first partner begins thinking about reconciliation, he finds his place has been taken, and the crucial opportunity for renewing the marriage passes. If you are serious about reconciliation, you must avoid all other exclusive relationships.

Another essential is to *admit your own faults and ask forgiveness*. You may feel that your partner has been much more to blame than you. But you too have contributed to the breakdown of the marriage. If you want reconciliation, you must not accuse him; keep yourself strongly in check to avoid this. Nor must you demand, or even expect, that he will immediately admit his faults and ask your forgiveness. That will have to come at some stage, but he may not be ready for it yet.

You need to take the initiative. God has made it quite clear that there can be no reconciliation in marriage without repentance and acknowledging that we have been at fault (see Jeremiah 3:12-14 – 'Return, faithless Israel . . . I will frown on you no longer. Only acknowledge your guilt . . . for I am your husband'). Asking forgiveness is the surest way of opening the possibility of reconciliation.

It is also helpful to *speak with hope about the future of your relationship*. 'Express hope and confidence that the two of you

can find answers to your past failures. Your hope will tend to
stimulate hope in your spouse . . . You cannot force reconciliation; you can only make the prospects look bright.'[51] If you
suggest moves towards reconciliation simply because you feel it
is your Christian duty but clearly believing that it will get
nowhere, then your expectations will be fulfilled. But if you are
able to gain hope from God, and gently express hope, reconciliation may seem to your partner like a more possible, and
more attractive, idea.

Remembering the good times and rich experiences you had
together will be important. This will give you the motivation to
work again at your marriage and may cause confidence to return
as you look to the future.

You will probably need to *say you would like to work towards
rebuilding your relationship*. Make it quite clear you know that
this could not happen all at once and that it would at times be
difficult for you both; that is why you are suggesting *working
towards* the rebuilding of your relationship. It is also not the re-
establishing of your old relationship that you are suggesting, but
working to create a new and better relationship.

Don't look for an immediate response to your suggestion.
Give him time to think it over, if he wants, and to reply when he
is ready.

He may say 'no'. That would be a bitter blow, especially as it
will probably have cost you a lot to admit your failings and ask
to work together on your relationship. You will probably have
prayed a lot about your suggestion and have a large emotional
investment in his agreeing to it. But despite the bitterness of the
disappointment, don't give up all hope. Stay in touch with your
partner as much as you can. You have made him a generous
offer; things may/will change and he may want to explore
whether the offer is still open.

If he says 'yes' to the suggestion, *allow time for the rebuilding
of the relationship*. Don't be in a rush, or grow impatient when
many difficulties remain or resurface. Richmond wisely says that

it took time for your marriage to get into a mess; it will take time to get out of it: 'You will be making progress as you work on your problems [probably with the help of a wise mutual friend or counsellor, who can be more objective] . . . over a period of months. It will be a two-steps-forward-and-one-step-back situation; so don't be overwhelmed if your recovery is not consistent. Measure your progress by the month, not by the day. Old, bad habits . . . are hard to break and you must give your mate the freedom to fail.'[52]

One particular area where patience and compromise may be needed is resuming sexual relations. Every couple is of course different, but quite often the man wants to have sex again immediately while the woman feels that many issues should be resolved before intercourse is even contemplated. This will need to be discussed and an unforced agreement reached. In many cases it is wise to leave sexual intercourse until later in the reconciliation process, when mutual sexual pleasure can be given ungrudgingly.

This leads to an important principle: *don't be walked over*. If your attitude is: 'You can come to me at any time, in any way; I won't ask any questions,' you will only earn your partner's contempt. James Dobson writes: '[To] say in effect: "No matter how badly you treat me, I'll still be here at your feet, because I can't survive without you" . . . is the best way . . . to kill' a relationship.[53] Where lasting reconciliation has been achieved it is always when both partners have played a full part in laying down new ground-rules and both partners have had to compromise.

It is necessary to *work out goals together*. If both partners want to work towards reconciliation, Richmond suggests that each separately should make a list of ten goals for the marriage. These should then be shared with the other partner and explained. Next, you and your partner should combine the two lists into one set of ten priorities. This process itself will clarify your vision for the future of your relationship and help you to work together. It is then important to agree on practical and concrete steps which you are able to take so as to make these goals a reality.[54]

It is often best to *do this work with the help of a wise person whom you both trust*. Of course it is possible to forge a way ahead without any outside help, but it is normally helpful to have a trusted friend or counsellor who can help to calm renewed anger and suggest possible solutions when a seeming impasse has been reached. Bob Burns suggests a variation on Richmond's approach (see the previous paragraph): Each partner should list his/her demands and expectations. Then both partners, with the help of a counsellor, can agree which of these demands and expectations are just and achievable. They can then be prioritised, in order of importance and in the order in which they can be expected to become reality. Then, still with the help of the counsellor, the couple can work on a *loose* timetable of when and how these expectations might be realised; and the couple, with the counsellor, can regularly evaluate how the timetable is working out in practice.[55]

Especially if you are able eventually to renew your marriage, *you will need the continuing support of your friends*. Once a couple are reunited, people often assume that all their problems have been solved. In fact, there are likely to be continuing difficulties and days, or weeks, when you think seriously about separating again. You will need to ask for the continuing prayers, support and counsel of your friends.

In all this, it is essential to *remember that what you are working towards is a new relationship*. If you try to return to the relationship you had before, you will make the same mistakes and separate again, with increased disillusionment and pain. You must both be entirely clear that you are seeking a quite new and better-founded relationship. 'Reconciliation demands a choice. It is a choice against continued separation and . . . divorce. It is a choice to reaffirm your marital vows and actively seek to rediscover . . . [what] God had in mind when he instituted marriage. It is not a choice to go back to the kind of relationship you had when you separated, but to work towards establishing something far more meaningful.'[56]

Paul's words about progress in the Christian life are especially apt when reconciliation is being sought: 'You were taught, with regard to your former way of life, to put off your old self, . . . to be made new in the attitude of your minds, and to put on the new self, created to be like God in true righteousness and holiness' (Ephesians 4:22-24).

This points to the most vital motive of all. If you are able to work towards reconciliation, *remember that you are pleasing God and imitating God.* Paul describes God's work to save the world like this: 'God was reconciling the world to himself in Christ, not counting men's sins against them' (2 Corinthians 5:19). Of course your partner has sinned against you; of course he has hurt you deeply again and again, he has devastated your life. But if you can learn gradually not to hold those sins against him, and if you can actively work towards as much reconciliation as possible, you will be imitating the God who turned in love to you and gave himself in renewed commitment to you.

Key verses

'Blessed are the peacemakers, for they will be called sons of God' (Matthew 5:9).
'The Lord said to me, "Go, show your love to your wife again"' (Hosea 3:1).

CHAPTER 11

CHRIST'S POWER IN WEAKNESS

Charles and Stephanie were deeply involved in both church and community. Charles was an elder of the Baptist Church and an occasional preacher; he was also a much respected GP. Stephanie was his supportive wife and mother of their five children. She was an assistant leader in one section of the Sunday school.

The medical practice took on a young female doctor. Charles began an affair with her, and over the next eighteen months vacillated between leaving his wife and breaking off the affair.

Stephanie was devastated. She spoke to her minister but felt she could tell no one else, not even her own parents. Her health deteriorated rapidly and her weight dropped to under six stone. The children began to be neglected. She came very close to a complete breakdown and was admitted to a psychiatric hospital for a time. God seemed nowhere near. She said to her minister, 'I know there is a God. I know there is Jesus, the Son of God. But he and I are not in the same orbit.'

This is one story, a true story which, like all the others in this book, has had some details changed to preserve anonymity. Your story is different. Every story is different. But there are common factors. Severe marriage difficulties, separation or divorce leave us feeling weak: physically weak, emotionally weak, spiritually weak. What does God have to say to us in our weakness?

In 2 Corinthians 12, Paul tells us of a remarkable experience of Christ he had been given fourteen years earlier. The account is tantalisingly brief because he does not want to dwell on this powerful experience (vv. 1-6). Rather, he wants to speak about his own weakness and how God met him in it:

> [7]To keep me from becoming conceited because of these surpassingly great revelations, there was given me a thorn in my flesh, a messenger of Satan, to torment me. [8]Three times I pleaded with the Lord to take it away from me. [9]But he said to me, 'My grace is sufficient for you, for my power is made perfect in weakness.' Therefore I will boast all the more gladly about my weaknesses, so that Christ's power may rest on me. [10]That is why, for Christ's sake, I delight in weaknesses, in insults, in hardships, in persecutions, in difficulties. For when I am weak, then I am strong. (2 Corinthians 12:7-10)

The final chapter of this book is an attempt to expound this passage and to illustrate it from the life of Stephanie and others.

A thorn in the flesh

Something happened to Paul which caused him great pain and left him feeling weak and helpless. Some scholars suggest it was an illness: perhaps recurrent malaria (compare 2 Corinthians 1:8-11) or partial blindness (compare Galatians 4:13-15; 6:11) or a severe speech impediment (compare 2 Corinthians 10:9,10). Some think it may have been the opponents who were implacably opposed to him (compare 2 Corinthians 11:13-15). It has even been suggested that his thorn in the flesh was a very difficult marriage relationship or a divorce that went back several years.

The truth is that we don't know. And perhaps that is a help to us, allowing us to identify with Paul, even though our situation may be different from his. Every reader for whom this book is written will have his or her own thorn in the flesh. It may be a marriage which drains you of all energy and self-esteem; the only times of relief and happiness are when your partner is away from home. It may be a divorce which you didn't want and which has caused you deep pain. It may be a separation which you did want but which has turned out to be much more difficult than you had imagined.

A messenger of Satan

Paul called his thorn in the flesh 'a messenger of Satan' (2 Corinthians 12:7). Somewhere behind all suffering and evil in the world is Satan. It has been so from the beginning (Genesis 3:1-5; compare Revelation 12:9; John 8:44). Paul says that Satan, in inflicting on him this thorn in the flesh, desired only 'to torment me' (2 Corinthians 12:7); the Greek word most normally means 'to beat me about the head'.

Marriage difficulties are an evil. Separation and divorce are evils. This does not mean that divorce is always a wrong course of action. Christ made it quite clear that God permits us to divorce when our partner has been sexually unfaithful and when we can as a result of the adultery no longer bear to remain within the marriage (Matthew 5:32; 19:9). Paul says that we may agree to (not initiate) a divorce when a non-Christian partner insists on it (1 Corinthians 7:15).

But marriage problems, separation and divorce are still evils. Behind them is the prince of evil. He is the enemy of marriages (those whom 'God has joined together': Mark 10:9; Matthew 19:6); he is our enemy. The very word 'Satan' means 'adversary'. His desire is to 'torment' us, to beat us up emotionally.

Given by God

The paradox is that the 'thorn in the flesh' is not only 'a messenger of Satan' but given by God. Paul says, 'To keep me from becoming conceited because of these surpassingly great

revelations, there was given me a thorn in my flesh'
(2 Corinthians 12:7). He can only mean: given by God. This is
proved not only by the fact that the phrase 'was given' would
naturally be understood by a New Testament reader as 'was
given by God' (compare e.g. Ephesians 3:8; 6:19), but especially
because the purpose of this 'gift' was 'to keep me from becoming
conceited'. The squashing of pride could not be a purpose of
Satan (compare 1 Timothy 3:6), but it is one of the purposes of
God (see Deuteronomy 8:2,3).

So the thorn in the flesh was given by God. This is what
causes us as Christians such confusion. In the midst of the pain
of our marriage problems or our divorce, we cry out, 'Why have
you let this happen to me? It's so evil. It has the fingerprints of
Satan all over it. So why didn't you stop it?' Paul doesn't answer
that question. He simply states that his thorn in the flesh was
both a messenger of Satan *and* given to him by God.

There is so much we don't understand when our marriage
breaks apart, but we know both these facts are true. We and our
circumstances are very much in the grip of evil; yet somehow –
in a way we don't understand and sometimes makes us very
angry with him – God is still in ultimate control. Certainly he
has allowed it to happen. But more than that: this new situation
is in some obscure way 'given' to us by God.

This fact confuses us. But it is also the source of our hopes. If
God was not somewhere in this, if God had really abandoned
us, there would be no possibility of hope. It is because this mess
has somehow been 'given' to us by God that we can retain any
sense of hope. Satan may have his purposes for us ('to torment
me', [v. 7]) but God has his purposes also. In Paul's case it was
'to keep me from becoming conceited' (twice in verse 7; so
accurately RSV). In our case the purpose will almost certainly be
different, but it is the fact that our new circumstances are given
by God which ensures that God has his purposes in it.

One man wrote to me: 'My wife left me fifteen months ago,
just before what would have been our fortieth wedding anni-

versary. She told me she had "known" Clive for thirty years. To say I was shattered is an understatement. But I have always known strength in our Lord and in his word. I strongly believe in Romans 8:28. So, I reasoned, God had a purpose in what happened and would guide me safely if I put all my trust in him. I did . . . Though emotionally I still feel very shaky, the past year has been a time of tremendous strength and growth.'

Insults, hardships, persecutions, difficulties

Paul expands on what God's purpose was for his life. But before we come to that, we should realise that Paul's sufferings were many and various. There was not just the thorn in the flesh (v. 7) but also 'insults . . . hardships . . . persecutions . . . difficulties' (v. 10).

You may have experienced all of these. Insults: your partner may have made the most cruel remarks while the marriage was still intact; Gerald's wife kept saying to him, 'It's been eighteen years of misery.' There may have been painful and insulting accusations about you made to the courts at the time of your divorce.

Hardships: especially financial. So many divorcees find that money suddenly becomes extraordinarily tight; that they and the children have to do without; that they run up debts from which their parents or friends have to bail them out.

Persecutions: the most painful of all are when you feel that the children are being poisoned against you.

Difficulties: the Greek word means literally 'narrow places'. It can seem as if life is closing in on you and that most of the opportunities and privileges which married couples enjoy are no longer open to you.

Weakness

But one word dominates in this passage: weakness (v. 9: weakness, my weaknesses; v. 10: weaknesses, I am weak). Paul felt weak, and knew that Christ had been weak (2 Corinthians 13:4).

Any doctor will vouch that physical weakness is very common during and after marriage breakup: splitting headaches (as mentioned above, 'torment' [v. 7] means 'beat about the head'), loss of weight and appetite, exhaustion, being vulnerable to disease. Stephanie's health went right downhill and she was constantly on tablets.

We are also emotionally weak: easily knocked off balance, impatient with the children, angry, bitter, eaten up by guilt, depressed; needing to talk and talk and talk, yet very conscious that friends may begin to drop us if we can't stop dwelling on our troubles.

Most Christians are acutely aware that they are spiritually weak: God has disappeared; their spiritual life has disappeared; they find it hard to come to worship or to be with other Christians. Stephanie immediately dropped out of her house group because she couldn't face the people who knew Charles and her so well.

Pleading with Christ

'Three times I pleaded with the Lord to take it away' (v. 8). Paul couldn't bear this thorn in the flesh; it was evil ('a messenger of Satan') and it was desperately painful. He begged Christ to take it away. It seems he prayed for a time and then (for whatever reason) stopped; and then started praying again. He had three periods of intense praying about his 'thorn'.

Many of us have gone through periods of earnest praying about our marriage. We have prayed very hard for a time, and perhaps asked others to pray. Then things have got better (and we saw it as an answer to prayer), or we've got used to the pain and it hasn't bothered us so much, or we've seen no change and just given up on prayer. So we've stopped. But then something has happened – things have got worse or our hopes have been raised – and has triggered off our praying again.

We have prayed that the marriage will keep going and be healed. We have prayed that our partner will come back. We have prayed that we will be able to cope better emotionally.

Many of these marriage-related prayers are answered. There must be thousands of marriages, hundreds of thousands throughout the world, that have been saved and rebuilt in answer to prayer.

But Paul's prayer was not answered in the way he hoped. And that can be our experience too. Stephanie told me: 'I prayed and prayed. I read over and over again the parable of the lost sheep. I couldn't understand it: "Why isn't God searching for him and bringing him back?" I took it for granted that I was praying and the Lord would make it right. We were both his children; the children were his children; and in that light I didn't see any reason why it shouldn't come back together.' Her husband didn't come back.

Christ's answer

Yet Christ did answer Stephanie; and he did answer Paul. Paul prayed. He also listened. He knew enough about Christ to listen out for an answer which might be different from what he expected. And Christ did answer. In fact the way the verb is expressed (literally: 'he *has* said to me', [v. 9]) shows that Christ's answer echoed in Paul's mind for the rest of his life.

Christ's answer to Paul is the same that he often wants to give to us: 'My grace is sufficient for you, for my power is made perfect in weakness' (v. 9). He says to us: 'I've heard your prayer. I've been listening every time you've prayed. I'm not going to take away your weakness. Instead, I'm going to give you all the grace you need; all the help, the courage, the support, as a gift to you because I love you. And in your weakness – not in your strength but in your weakness – you will experience my power brought to perfection. This power of mine you could never experience if I did what you asked and took away the weakness you feel so deeply.'

You have prayed to Christ about your marriage, about your own feeling of desperation. But have you listened? We say, 'I've prayed but God hasn't answered.' Is that because we were screaming with pain and therefore deaf to any answer except the only one we wanted?

Keep praying. But also listen. Even if it is not what we hope to hear, let Christ's loving, reassuring answer sink in: 'My grace is sufficient for you, for my power is made perfect in weakness.'

Christ's power experienced

This is not just a promise which Christ gives. It is Paul's experience. Having listened to Christ's answer, and experienced Christ's power in his weakness, he is able to say, 'Therefore I will boast all the more gladly about my weaknesses, so that Christ's power may rest on me' (v. 9). It is not just that Christ's power is with him for a moment and then is gone again. Rather the power of Christ 'rests on him', making its home with him.

He continues to feel weak. But he can sum up all his experience in a paradoxical sentence: 'When I am weak, then I am strong' (v. 10).

In my twenties I came to know a widow very well. Bereaved in middle age, and without children, her whole life had fallen apart. She had given up her job because she couldn't cope with it any more. But in the dark pit of her grief she had become a committed Christian. She excitedly discovered the joy of Christ and of the Christian family. She could have gone back to work but decided not to, in order to serve Christ more single-mindedly. The result was that she had very little money.

One day we were talking about money and I said, rather insensitively, how reassuring it felt to have some savings in the bank. She turned to me and said very naturally, 'But you are deprived of really trusting in the Lord. When you have nothing to fall back on you can learn how faithful he is.' Her words struck me forcefully at the time, and I've never forgotten them.

Divorcees normally lose a great deal: their partner, financial security, self-esteem, sexual fulfilment, emotional equilibrium, friends – the list goes on and on. They are weak and vulnerable. But in that weakness they can experience the strength that Christ brings and learn how faithful he is.

His love can be experienced in prayer and in quietly listening to him. Stephanie told me how helpful the Psalms had been (for their realism) and Isaiah 53-55 (for their reassurance that God is in control, in spite of suffering).

We also experience his power through the friendship of Christians. Some time after his divorce, and probably as a result of it, Stan became a Christian. This was how he expressed his experience: 'I'm not out on a limb so much as a Christian. As a non-Christian I felt it far, far more. My non-Christian friends didn't realise how lonely one can get. They didn't think. I've had far more love, support and encouragement as a Christian.'

Delighting in weakness

Paul's conclusions from his experience are remarkable. 'Therefore I will *boast* all the more gladly about my weaknesses, so that Christ's power may rest upon me' (v. 9). 'That is why, for Christ's sake, I *delight* in weaknesses, in insults, in hardships, in persecutions, in difficulties. For when I am weak, then I am strong' (v. 10).

It seems extraordinary to say that you can 'boast about' (which means, here, 'be genuinely glad about') your weaknesses, or that you can 'delight in' them. Paul can say this not because weaknesses are good in themselves, but because they open up experiences of God's power. This is God's ultimate purpose in 'giving' (v. 7) him his thorn in the flesh: not just 'to keep me from becoming conceited' (v. 7) but 'so that Christ's power may rest on me' (v. 9).

No one expects you at the time your marriage is breaking up, or when the divorce comes through, to 'delight in' your weakness. But will God ever be able to lead you to that point? It all depends on how you react. The experience of divorce never leaves us the same in our relationship with Christ. We either become bitter and resentful; and we will then suddenly or gradually move away from Christ. Or we will struggle to be open to God, to listen to him; and he will then draw us deeper into the love of Christ and the knowledge of Christ.

Our church in Crowborough, like many churches throughout the western world, is full of people who have been divorced. Many of them have, through their experience of divorce, found Christ for the first time; others have grown substantially in their experience of Christ. One man put it very simply: 'After thirty-three years of marriage my wife decided to leave. Of course I have been crushed by this but I must say how much closer to the Lord I have been drawn.'

Many Christians – particularly, but not only, if they have worked through to reconciliation – are able to say, 'I am so grateful for the whole experience of the breakdown of our marriage. Not in itself; it was awful. But because of all that God has done through it, and how much I have come to know his power in my life.'

This chapter began with Stephanie. Her marriage broke up fifteen years ago. It is still painful for her to talk about it. But when I asked her if we could talk about the way her relationship with Christ has changed through it she readily, and even joyfully, agreed.

She was quite honest about how her spiritual life had initially gone to pieces. 'I found that I was more and more estranged from God, from Jesus', and she didn't want to be with Christian friends.

But she never stopped praying 'and – which was very

important – I never lost my desire to get back to God. I was always searching'. She didn't feel she could cope with reading much, but she read a few verses from the Bible and read a few Christian books (for example, one on prayer: 'because it was in short sections, I was able to take them in'). 'Slowly I began to draw closer to the Lord . . . I began slowly to see that the Lord really loved me.'

Fifteen years on she can say, 'He has given me a fulfilled life in many ways and brought me a great deal of happiness.' I asked her how her relationship with Christ had changed. She particularly emphasised two ways.

'It's now a far deeper relationship. Although I would have said before the divorce that I was sure of him, I now have the absolute certainty that *whatever* happens he is there with me . . . I know now that whatever happens, however dark the tunnel, the Lord will always take me through. He's there taking me through even if I don't see him at the time.' Looking back over the period of her marriage breakup and divorce: 'I came to see that he had been there all the time. But I hadn't noticed. He hadn't let me go, me or mine. That gave me a security that is beyond all knowing.'

That conviction was tested ten years later when one of Stephanie's children had a car crash and was completely paralysed. A few weeks later, perhaps partly because of this accident, Stephanie's mother died of a heart attack (her father was already dead). Stephanie was devastated, but she never sank anywhere near as low as at the time of her divorce. She had learned that Christ is with her and multiplies his love to her in the darkest times.

The other way in which her relationship with Christ has changed she expressed like this: 'I think that there is a sense in which being on your own enables you to be more single-minded in your love for the Lord. Although I would still rather have my marriage, there are things within a marriage that can keep you away from the Lord. You can put him aside more easily. You can

make the other person more important than the Lord . . . Now
I'm very close to several of my friends, but even if my husband
were to die and I remarried, I think the Lord would still come
first.' Why? 'Because of the deeper knowledge of the Lord I have
now; what I have learned of him. How could I before that have
known his utter reliability? I hadn't experienced such a time of
darkness before.'

Key verse

'He said to me, "My grace is sufficient for you, for my power is
made perfect in weakness"' (2 Corinthians 12:9).

NOTES

1 Westermann, C., *Isaiah 40-66 – A Commentary. Old Testament Library* (SCM: London, 1969), p. 96.

2 North, C. R., *The Second Isaiah: Introduction, Translation and Commentary to Chapters 40-55* (OUP: Oxford, 1964), p. 38.

3 Motyer, J. A., *The Prophecy of Isaiah* (IVP: Leicester, 1993), p. 320.

4 Bauer, E., Arndt, W. F., Gingrich, F. W. and Danker, F., *Greek-English Lexicon of the New Testament* (University of Chicago: Chicago, IL, 1979²).

5 Compston, C., *Recovering from Divorce* (Hodder and Stoughton: London, 1993).

6 *Ibid.,* pp. 86,87.

7 Wallerstein, J. S. and Kelly, J. B., *Surviving the Breakup: How Children and Parents Cope with Divorce* (Basic Books: New York, 1980), p. 225.

8 *Ibid.,* p. 10.

9 *Ibid.,* pp. 202,211,212,309.

10 *Ibid.,* p. 306.

11 Dominian, J., *Marital Breakdown* (Penguin: Harmondsworth, 1968), pp. 122-127.

12 Wallerstein, J. S. and Kelly, J. B., *op.cit.,* p. 292.

13 Compston, C., *op.cit.,* p. 91.

14 Jones, T., *The Single Again Handbook* (Nelson: Nashville, TN, 1993), p. 3.

15 *Ibid.,* p. xii.

16 Compston, C., *op.cit.,* p. 62.

17 Wallerstein, J. S. and Kelly, J. B., *op.cit.,* p. 153.

18 *Ibid.,* pp. 190,194,195.

19 Green, W., *The Christian and Divorce* (Mowbray: London, 1981), p. 97.

20 Hosier, H. K., *To Love Again* (Abingdon: Nashville, TN, 1985), pp. 140,141.

21 Wallerstein, J. S. and Kelly, J. B., *op.cit.,* p. 307.

22 Craigie, P., *Psalms 1-50. Word Biblical Commentary* (Word: Waco, TX, 1983), p. 74.

23 Cornes, A. C. J., *Divorce and Remarriage: Biblical Principles and Pastoral Practice* (Hodder and Stoughton: London, 1993), pp. 272-276.

24 See Haskey, J., 'The Proportion of Married Couples Who Divorce: Past Patterns and Current Prospects', *Population Trends* 83 (1996), pp. 25-36.

John Haskey, principal marriage statistician at the Government Office for National Statistics, calculates that 41% of all marriages contracted in 1993-94 will end in divorce if divorce rates persist unchanged at their 1993-94 levels (in fact, the divorce rate has been rising at about 1% per annum since around 1980). This figure is a percentage of all those marrying, whether for the first time or for a second or subsequent time.

Turning to second marriages, Haskey gives detailed figures for the years between 1951 and 1989. Comparing people who married for the first time at a certain age with those who remarried at the same age, remarriages after divorce were twice as likely to end in divorce for those married before 1961, and between one and a half and two times more likely to end in divorce for those married between 1961 and 1989.

25 Jones, T., *op.cit.,* p. 3.

26 Taylor, R., *Single and Whole* (IVP: Downers Grove, IL, 1984), p. 73.

27 Lagrange, M-J., *Évangile selon S. Matthieu. Études Bibliques* (Gabalda: Paris, 1923), p. 371.

28 Jones, T., *op.cit.,* p. 114.

29 Quoist, M., *Prayers of Life* (Gill and Macmillan: Dublin, 1963), p. 51, quoted in Evening, M., *Who Walk Alone: A Consideration of the Single Life* (Hodder and Stoughton: London, 1974), pp. 124,218.

30 Lewis, C. S., *Mere Christianity* (Collins: London, 1952), p. 85.

31 *Fresh Start* (Fresh Start Seminars: Wayne, PA, c.1983), p. 69.

32 Jones, T., *op.cit.,* p. 34.

33 Chapman, G., *Hope for the Separated* (Moody: Chicago, IL, 1982), p. 25.

34 *Fresh Start* (tape): *Re-entry into the Single Life.*

35 Jones, T., *op.cit.,* p. 146.

36 Evening, M., *op.cit.,* pp. 200,201.

37 Rad, G. von, *Genesis. Old Testament Library* (SCM: London, 1972²), p. 84.

38 Crispin, K., *Divorce – The Forgivable Sin?* (Hodder and Stoughton: London, 1989), p. 170.

39 Jones, T., *Fresh Start* (tape): *Working through Bitterness and Learning to Forgive.*

40 Huggett, J., *Marriage on the Mend* (Kingsway: Eastbourne, 1987), p. 129.

41 Chapman, G., *Now That You Are Single Again* (Here's Life: San Bernardino, CA, 1985), p. 35.

42 Lewis, C. S., quoted in Wilson, R. F., 'Don't Pay the Price of Counterfeit Forgiveness', *Moody Magazine,* October 1985.

43 Huggett, J., *op.cit.,* p. 132.

44 Chapman, G., *Hope for the Separated,* p. 15.

45 *Ibid.,* p. 98.

46 *Ibid.,* p. 12.

47 *Ibid.,* p. 61,62.

48 *Ibid.,* pp. 62,63.

49 Talley, J., *Reconcilable Differences* (Nelson: Nashville, TN, 1991), p. 137.

50 *Ibid.,* p. 13.

51 Chapman, G., *Hope for the Separated,* p. 25.

52 Richmond, G., *The Divorce Decision* (Word: Waco, TX, 1988), p. 171.

53 Dobson, J., *Man to Man about Women* (Kingsway: Eastbourne, 1976), p. 78ff.

54 Richmond, G., *op.cit.,* pp. 180-183.

55 *Fresh Start* (tape): *The Separation and Reconciliation Struggle.*

56 Chapman, G., *Hope for the Separated,* p. 88.

BIBLIOGRAPHY

This bibliography is confined exclusively to works quoted in the text. For a fuller bibliography see my earlier book, *Divorce and Remarriage.*

Bauer, E., Arndt, W. F., Gingrich, F. W. and Danker, F., *Greek-English Lexicon of the New Testament* (University of Chicago: Chicago, IL, 1979²).

Lord Chancellor's Department, *Looking to the Future: Mediation and the Ground for Divorce* (HMSO: London, 1995).

Chapman, G., *Hope for the Separated* (Moody: Chicago, IL, 1982).

Chapman, G., *Now that You Are Single Again* (Here's Life: San Bernardino, CA, 1985).

Compston, C., *Recovering from Divorce* (Hodder and Stoughton: London, 1993).

Cornes, A. C. J., *Divorce and Remarriage: Biblical Principles and Pastoral Practice* (Hodder and Stoughton: London, 1993).

Craigie, P., *Psalms 1-50,* Word Biblical Commentary (Word: Waco, TX, 1983).

Crispin, K., *Divorce – The Forgivable Sin?* (Hodder and Stoughton: London, 1989).

Dobson, J., *Man to Man about Women.* (Kingsway: Eastbourne, 1976).

Dominian, J., *Marital Breakdown* (Penguin: Harmondsworth, 1968).

Evening, M., *Who Walk Alone: A Consideration of the Single Life* (Hodder and Stoughton: London, 1974).

Wayne, P. A., *Fresh Start* (Fresh Start Seminars: c. 1983).

Genesis Rabbah: The Judaic Commentary to the Book of Genesis, Volume 1: 1:1-8:14. (Scholars: ET. Atlanta, 1985).

Goudge, E., *The Dean's Watch* (Hodder and Stoughton: London).

Green, W., *The Christian and Divorce* (Mowbray: London, 1981).

Haskey, J., 'The proportion of married couples who divorce: past patterns and current prospects' in *Population Trends* 83 (1996) pp 25-36.

Hosier, H. K., *To Love Again* (Abingdon: Nashville, TN, 1985).

Huggett, J., *Marriage on the Mend* (Kingsway: Eastbourne, 1987).

Jones, T., *The Single Again Handbook* (Nelson: Nashville, TN, 1993).

Lagrange, M-J., *Évangile Selon S. Matthieu. Études Bibliques* (Gabalda: Paris, 1923).

Lewis, C. S., *Mere Christianity* (Collins: London, 1952).

Motyer, J. A., *The Prophecy of Isaiah* (IVP: Leicester, 1993).

North, C. R., *The Second Isaiah: Introduction, Translation and Commentary to Chapters 40-55* (OUP: Oxford, 1964).

Quoist, M., *Prayers of Life* (Gill and Macmillan: ET. Dublin, 1963).

Rad, G. von, *Genesis* Old Testament Library (SCM: ET. London, 1972[2]).

Richmond, G., *The Divorce Decision* (Word: Waco, TX, 1988).

Talley, J., *Reconcilable Differences* (Nelson: Nashville, TN, 1991).

Taylor, R., *Single and Whole* (IVP: Downers Grove, IL, 1984).

Wallerstein, J. S. and Kelly, J. B., *Surviving the Breakup: How children and parents cope with divorce* (Basic Books: New York, 1980).

Westermann, C., *Isaiah 40–66 – A Commentary* Old Testament Library (SCM: ET. London, 1969).

Wilson, R. F., 'Don't pay the price of counterfeit forgiveness' in *Moody Magazine,* October 1985.